Silas

A Victorian Rural Postman

His Life and Times

by Alan Stone

Published in 2006 by
Shepton Mallet Local History Group
10 Society Road, Shepton Mallet. Somerset BA4 5GF

email: sheptonhistory@btinternet.com

Printed by Creeds the Printers, Broadoak, Bridport, Dorset DT6 5NL

ISBN 978-0-9548125-3-9

Contents

Cover - background photograph from Pennard Hill looking towards Wraxall
Photograph and cover design Richard Stone

Foreword

The story of the life and career of Silas Davis epitomizes the Victorian concepts of duty and service to a remarkable degree; it also provides a glimpse of what to many must seem an enduring rustic idyll - yet even Silas in his long life was to see how transient a feature this ordered society was, for he witnessed the germination, flowering and slow withering of a part of the great Victorian social experiment.

East Pennard and Pylle, the rural parishes served by Silas, can be to a great extent portrayed in the now politically incorrect verse of the popular Victorian hymn 'All things bright and beautiful' by Mrs. Alexander;-

> "The rich man in his castle,
> The poor man at his gate,
> God made them, high or lowly,
> And order'd their estate."

The timeless tranquility of these villages has survived surprisingly well since Silas's day (apart from along the length of the A37!), with minimal development taking place during the twentieth century. Both were 'estate' villages, and in their present form largely a Victorian adaptation of their earlier layout. Pylle was a very small, if original, part of the very large Portman Estate, with no resident squire, but all the other features of a typical estate village - large tenanted commercial farms and 'model' cottages, a school and church all provided by the Portmans. East Pennard, a much larger parish including numerous hamlets, contained many yeoman farmers in addition to the more modest Napier estate, which during Silas's youth had largely transformed the village itself to create an idealized patrician landscape with 'model' cottages erected in place of dilapidated hovels, and ranges of substantial farm buildings provided on the numerous farmsteads. Both villages had recently erected imposing rectories, and commodious new schools appeared at the beginning of Silas's period of employment.

The re-structuring of the physical landscape was, however, only one side of the coin. The other was the 'improvement' of the population, by means not only of the upgraded accommodation, but also by compulsory education, and the almost obligatory attendance at church and Sunday school. Village society became rigidly stratified and ordered. It was this environment that to Silas must have seemed so permanent and solid - yet the story of his life reveals just how transient it was. In his youth he witnessed the desperate poverty resulting from the decayed textile industries of Shepton Mallet; in contrast he would have come across the impeccably liveried flunkeys at East Pennard. These villages were never to be more prosperous or immaculately cared for than in the decades of Silas's service. Soon after his retirement, however, came the cataclysm of the Great War - with numerous casualties from the communities Silas had served. Agricultural depression, and with it the sale of the Portman estate at Pylle was to follow - the Napier estate at East Pennard being sold six years after Silas's death. The internal combustion engine, aircraft and electricity had all appeared and were transforming Silas's world at an ever increasing rate. We can only guess at his reactions.

Alan Stone, in his own inimitable style, has brought this era to life with his story of the remarkable career of this most conscientious public servant, and thereby has provided yet another insight into an obscure area of local history - its perusal is both a rewarding and informative experience.

Adrian V Pearse M.A.(Oxen)
Farmer and Local Historian

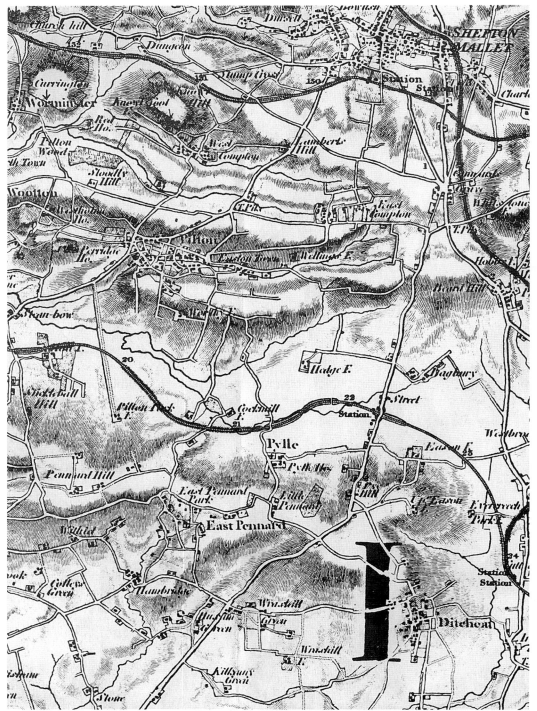

Reproduced from 1890 Ordnance Survey map with kind permision of the Ordnance Survey

Silas - A Victorian Rural Postman - introduction

One of the joys of doing historical research in local newspapers is that you never know what you are going to come across. As part of a Local History Group project I was investigating Shepton Mallet during the Second World War by going week by week through the local paper for that time. In October 1942 I came across the obituary below which straight away grabbed the imagination.

'9 October 1942. Death of Mr Silas Davis'

By the passing on Saturday of Mr Silas Davis, at the advanced age of 93 years, the town has lost one of its most esteemed and picturesque residents. With advancing years, and failing sight, he had not for the past two or three years been the familiar figure in the town of former years. Before that time, however, he loved to stroll up into the town, and would enjoy an hour amongst old friends in the Constitutional Club; where it was a rare treat to catch him in reminiscent vein. He loved to talk of bygone times, and to tell of some thrill encountered upon his rounds during his 40 years meritorious service as a Rural Postman. His daily round was from the Town Post Office to Pylle, East Pennard and Wraxall, returning to East Pennard, Pylle Post Office and Shepton Mallet - 17 miles. It is estimated that during his service he walked 246,000 miles. He delivered letters every day of the week, including Sundays, taking every other Sunday off. Mr Davis retired 33 years ago, and since then has made himself useful in a number of ways. His retirement was marked by the Post Office in befitting fashion, and he was the proud holder of numerous service decorations and bars. By his death, the town has lost a charming personality, one who bubbled over with good cheer and generosity, and who was always a pleasure to meet. He leaves three sons and three daughters, besides numerous grandchildren and great grandchildren to mourn his loss.

The Funeral

Mr Davis was accorded a full postman's funeral on Wednesday afternoon, when he was borne to his last resting place by four members of the postal staff.

The family mourners were:- Mr and Mrs J B Godfrey, and Mr and Mrs Axe, daughters and son-in-laws; Mrs H Harris, daughter; Mr and Mrs E H Davis, son and daughter-in-law; Mr E B Davis and Master Norman Davis, grandsons.

Included in others present were Mr H Chamberlain, representing the Foresters. The following were the members of the Postal Staff attending; Messsrs H J Nunn, R H Allen, C Tripp and R Cooper, bearers; A Davis telegram messenger; retired

Silas Davis, Rural Postman (photo Christine Marshman / Barrie Davis)

PO Engineer Mr G Walshe; retired PO members from Evercreech and old colleagues, Mr Corry and Mr G Gifford. There were four representatives from East Pennard, including Messrs A L England and Cyril England, Mr W Cable, Auxiliary Postman, who is now serving with the Forces, was also able to be present.

The beautiful floral tributes were as follows;- In loving memory of dear Dad from Nancy and John. In loving memory of dear Dad from Allie. In loving memory of dear Dad from his loving son and daughter, Ern and May. In loving memory of dear Dad from Ern and Joe. In loving memory of dear Grandpa, from his loving Grand son Bernard, Evelyn and Great Grandsons Gorman, Graham and Barry. In remembrance of an old Comrade, from the Head Postmaster and Staff, Shepton Mallet. In loving memory of a true Friend and Brother officer of the AOF., from H Chamberlain. In affectionate remembrance, from T Clifford. In remembrance of an old neighbour, from Mrs Hayter, Stevenson, Harvey and Miss Fear.

The late Mr Davis, who joined the postal service under the late Mr Charles Fudge, is believed to be the first postman in Shepton Mallet to receive the Long Service medal - April 1908.

The funeral arrangements were carried out by Mr H Moon."

Mr Silas Davies was obviously an interesting man - he had walked the equivalent to more than 10 times around the world over 40 years across the same patch of rural Somerset. People just don't do things like that anymore. Imagine how well he must have known the countryside and the people in it.

Familiarity with the local newspaper made me realize straight away that this was no ordinary obituary. Reports of this length and detail were not given to the ordinary workers - even those soldiers dying in the war. This was the sort of obituary that was usually reserved for local dignitaries such as doctors or bank managers. The language of the report was also uncharacteristically profuse, almost gushing in extolling his virtues. It had to be concluded that Silas Davis was a significant local figure. Intriguing as well to see at the head of the list of mourners his son-in-law J B Godfrey. John Byrt Godfrey was a local farmer and a prominent local resident.

The disciplines of historic research dictated that I had to stick to the job I had in hand but I made a note to return to Silas at some time in the future. What more could I find out about the man and his background? Where did he and his family come from? What were the conditions in Shepton Mallet at this time? What was the Post Office like and how did it develop in the 40 year period he was working for it? How many pairs of boots did he wear out? Would it be possible to work out where he went, to reconstruct his round? Could you investigate the countryside and farming of the period to find out what he would have seen around him in the fields and hamlets? Could you find out more about the people he was delivering to and would have met on his rounds? How has society changed since those days - for better or worse?

The period when Silas was treading his extensive round is commonly referred to as the 'Great Agricultural Depression.' Social Historians seem split between those who emphasize rural poverty and the exodus of labour from the land on the one hand and on the other who want to paint a picture of a past rural arcadia worthy of nostalgia for a past age. What were the villages and hamlets that Silas delivered to really like? Were there grand houses or farms or industry or just rural cottagers?

These are the questions that I now set out with for this exercise. It has been amazing how many people I have met who have been able to add snippets of information and enabled me to build up quite a rounded picture of Silas, his life and times even though he retired nearly 100 years ago. I 'phoned local Shepton Mallet Town historian Fred Davis to check as to whether he was related. Fred had put a short piece and a photograph of Silas in one of his books on the town. 'No,' the answer came back - 'but I think a couple of his great grandsons are still alive. There is Gorman who lives somewhere in Whitstone Road and a Barrie somewhere in town.' Work with the telephone directory and a couple of speculative letters bought an amazingly quick response from both and yes they would be willing to talk to me. They were both sons of Bernard Davis who was a son of Ernest Howard Davis, the youngest son of Silas.

Gorman, nearing 80 had memories of sitting with Silas as an old man when he was a boy, and also poignant memories of his own time as a telegram boy in the last years of World War Two, the tragic reactions of mothers when delivered the telegrams notifying them of their sons' deaths.

Barrie who had only been two when his great grandfather died but had been close to his own father Bernard and had saved some pictures and artifacts of Silas. Now retired, Barrie had spent many years as an Insurance agent for the Pearl around central Somerset and over the years talking to many old rural characters has built up an incredible store of stories including some about Silas from people who knew him. Both Barrie and Gorman share a fascination with clocks which seems to be a family trait which as we will see probably started with Silas. There is also a third brother, Graham, still living in Shepton Mallet.

The mystery of John Byrt Godfrey was quickly cleared. I knew retired farmer John

Godfrey, his grandson, and bumped into him in the supermarket. Nancy - usually called Annie and Silas's second daughter was John Byrt Godfrey's second wife - so John was his step grandson. He could remember going to see Silas in his cottage behind the Crown Inn at the bottom of Cowl Street. It is through this connection that even a touch of our Royalty edges into Silas's tale.

In another co-incidence Barrie bumped into Christine Marshman and mentioned to her that I was interested in Silas. Christine is an active member of our Shepton Mallet Local History Group who has helped and is helping with a number of history projects we have undertaken. I discovered that she was a great granddaughter of Silas, through Silas's eldest daughter, the Mr and Mrs Axe who appear amongst the mourners in the obituary. Christine had some years earlier studied her family history and had copied of a number of certificates and photographs relevant to Silas.

My wife Christine, with nearly 30 years experience of family history studies, contributed her skills in tracing the family and identifying where they lived and what they did. Registers, censuses and old maps were used to find out more about Silas and the people he met on his round. Researches in the Shepton Mallet Journal added more detail about Silas - especially around his retirement in 1908. The history of the Post Office was delved into and a trip to the Post Office Archives in London revealed more detail about Silas.

It has been a fascinating journey of investigation and I hope I have managed to write it up in a way that will be of interest to many.

Silas and Shepton at the time of his birth.

What can we find out about the young Silas, his family and the town into which he was born on 26 February 1849? The first reference to Silas Davis that we have traced is in the 1851 census when he is recorded as a two year old living in Darshill as the then youngest member of a large family.

Delving back further the same family can be found on the 1841 Census - the earliest which gives names. In 1841 they were living in Coombe Lane - the narrow lane leading from West Shepton down a small steep valley with a tributary of the 'River Sheppy' coming out in front of Bowlish House at the bottom. On the right as you walk down the road today you can still see some small cottages. Some of these had been condemned in the 1940s and again in the 1980s but have since been restored to habitable standards. There is also a very recognizable old textile mill, one of very few still standing in Shepton. This one has survived by being converted into houses. In the steep hillside behind the mill there are still some tunnels where folk tradition suggests that silk worms for the silk industry where bred. This may seem questionable as it is most unlikely that sufficient mulberry leaves could be harvested locally. It is more likely that at the time of Silas's birth silk worm cocoons were stored here waiting for spinning - but there again it is always a risk challenging folk tradition.

By 1851 the family had moved only a few hundred yards down the valley of the Sheppy to Darshill. Here there are still traces and records of at least four textile mills, though how many would have still been in operation in 1850 is open to question. There are still many surviving old cottages - either in the valley bottom by the edge of the still traceable swampy millpond or built into the very steep north side of the valley beside the narrow lane as it climbs towards Ham.

The 1851 Census entry shows the following family:

John Davis	Head	56	Handloom Weaver	born Shepton Mallet
Mary Ann	Wife	42	Handloom Weaver	born Shepton Mallet
Thomas	son	16	Handloom Weaver	born Shepton Mallet
Ann	dau	15	Handloom Weaver	born Shepton Mallet
Mary	dau	12	Silk Factory	born Shepton Mallet
James	son	10	Silk Factory	born Shepton Mallet
Martha	dau	8		born Shepton Mallet
John	son	5		born Shepton Mallet
Silas	son	2		born Shepton Mallet

It would seem they had at least one more child as listed in the 1871 Census is an Albert Davis then aged 19 who was born on 3rd January 1852.

These bare facts start to paint a picture with which we can feed our imagination with the conventional images of what the novelists and social reformers of the day saw as grim Victorian industrialisation. We are conditioned to Dickensian scenes of long working hours with the whole family working in the factories - even the children; James at 10 is shown as a factory worker. A BBC period dramatisation would also suggest impoverished cottages, harsh overseers in the factories and the mill owners flaunting their wealth with an unremitting exploitation of the downtrodden workers. To add to this dark picture is the fact that Shepton Mallet was economically an extremely depressed town at this time.

The fact that James aged 10 is shown as a worker in a silk factory is extremely interesting. My wife who does a lot of family history transcription work on censuses, suggested that having a child that young working is most unusual at this time. An early Factory Act of the 1830s had already outlawed children under 12 working in factories but the silk industry had won an exemption as it was claimed that small hands were needed to work with the delicate silken threads. It is probable that this was an overstated picture and life would not have seemed quite so bad to those who grew up in it.

From the later mediaeval times until the end of the eighteenth century Shepton Mallet had been notable for its woollen industry. At various time it had been noted for colourful cloths but in the main it had just been noted for quantity. Along with Frome, Shepton represents the southern limits of the Cotswold's woollen industry which was based on the large numbers of sheep farmed locally and then, as machinery evolved, using the fast running local streams for power. It had probably reached its height over 100 years before and many of the richer 'manor' houses which can still be seen along the valley bottom running right through the town date from the first half of the eighteenth century. Many of the older large houses were also enlarged and refaced with Georgian splendour. For some reason the wealthy merchants and mill owners of Shepton at this period kept their grand homes near the mills and jumbled up amongst the workers' cottages; a distinctive feature of the town which can still be seen today. Edengrove in Leg Square and Bowlish House are the best examples of the new 'manors' that were built whilst Old Bowlish House and Whitstone House in Town Lane demonstrate how older houses were transformed.

However, by the latter part of the eighteenth century Shepton Mallet was losing out to the mills in Yorkshire where the 'Industrial Revolution' was underway with the use of steam powered new machinery on an altogether bigger scale than was seen in the south. Wool itself was also declining in relative importance to cotton,

Middle Mill at Darshill - likely work place of Silas's family.
To the right a tumble of small cottages built into the hillside. (photo Len Ware)

the raw material imported from the Americas, then spun and woven in the new factories of Lancashire. The mill owners in Shepton Mallet failed to keep up with these new developments, perhaps they did not like to change their traditional ways - although there is plenty of indication that new machinery was introduced. Perhaps the geography made large mills and transport difficult. It has also been suggested that local workers were particularly vigorous in their resistance to change. However it is beyond doubt that a decline set in. It was perhaps disguised for a while by the extra demand generated by the Napoleonic wars but by the end of the first two decades of the nineteenth century there had been an almost total collapse of the Shepton woollen industry and poverty was rife.

At the date of the first national census in 1801 the population of Shepton Mallet was over 5,000. Believe it or not Shepton was the fourth town in Somerset behind only Bath, Frome, and Taunton - in fact it was only a couple of hundred people behind Taunton - now the county town with approximately seven times the population of Shepton. The historian Collinson has claimed that there were over 4,000 people working in the eighteenth century woollen cloth industry however, it seems likely that this included the surrounding area. There is not much evidence that the population had declined significantly by 1801. An interesting feature of the town is that with minor swings up and down it did not significantly alter in size until after the Second World War. In the meantime many other towns such as Yeovil and Bridgwater and even Wells, Glastonbury, Street, Norton Radstock and

Chard had eclipsed Shepton in population terms during the nineteenth century.

The collapse of the traditional woollen industry threw the town into a severe economic depression in the 1820s. Pigot and Co's commercial Directory of 1830 says of the town

'...and comprises upwards of 20 streets and lanes; the principle streets are spacious and contain some well built dwellings; but the smaller ones are in general straggling, narrow, irregular and dirty.... This place at one time was very considerably engaged in the manufacture of broad and narrow woollen cloths and kerseymeres; but at present this trade is exceedingly depressed having been severely injured by the manufactories of Yorkshire:"

However it would be a mistake to suppose that the town was as dark and depressed by the time that Silas was born. Another directory, Hunts, of 1850 paints an altogether more optimistic picture of the town that Silas would have just been born into.

'The town is famed for the longevity of its inhabitants; the principle streets are spacious, and many of its buildings are modern erections; it is well lighted and drained; indeed few towns have been improved so much as this during the last 20 years.'

Of the town's industry Hunt's says:

'..and was at an early period of English history a town of considerable importance being extensively engaged in the manufacturing of woollen cloths and fine knit hose, the latter of which is still continued in the town and neighbourhood; but the principal manufactures at present carried on are crepe and silk velvet - these articles rank high in public estimation, both for their superior quality and beautiful appearance.'

Even allowing for a copywriter's enthusiasm in describing the town it can be seen that the town was moving forward. Waterloo Road - at first just called New Road had been built over its massive bridge running north out of the town towards Bristol in the 1830s. There was already a gasworks in the town which presumably provided some street lighting. During Silas's childhood the new road to Wells was cut down beside Darshill - Silas probably had a good view of the rough navvies as they cut the road through the rock on the south side of the valley. Perhaps as a toddler his brother would have led him across to see some of the fossils that the road makers were finding in the rocks. A few years later Silas would have joined in the excitement as the railway arrived in the town at Townsend and the whole town came out to celebrate in an enthusiastic style for the biggest party the town had ever seen.

It is also quite likely that Silas's family was not as hard up as many. The handloom weaver was considered at least a semi-skilled job and there is a suggestion that there was a certain amount of pride in good work. With so many of the family working they must have had sufficient income to be comfortable. His father almost certainly worked for the Darshill Mill that was listed in 1842 under Silk Throwsters as William Hardisty and Co (& Crepe manufacturers) Darshill. There was also a Hardisty Brothers at Kilver Street, a Peter Samuels at Croscombe and a John Braden in Leg St. It is possible to estimate from the 1841 census that between them they were then employing well over 1,000 workers. By 1852 the business had changed hands and was listed as Wm Phillips (& velvet) Draycott & Darshill. There was still a Hardisty Brothers at Kilver Street.

Davis, despite its Welsh sounding origins seems to have very much been a local name - as it still is, including a number of families in the town and some farming families in the surrounding area. The 1852 Slater's Directory identifies a number. Although it is impossible to work out any family connections it is interesting to see in that amongst gentry and clergy listed there is a Henry Davis Esq at Oakhill and a Rev John Davis also at Oakhill. These were probably not relatives, people of these classes tended to be more mobile and were not necessarily born locally. Also listed in Shepton and more likely to be related somewhere along the way are two bakers - Isaac Davis, Peter Street and James Davis, Town Lane - Samuel Davis of Town Street a grocer, Henry Davis, Garston Street, retailer of beer, William Davis a wheelwright in Kilver Street and John Davis a cork cutter in Town Street.

Although Shepton was clearly an industrial town it should also be recognized that the distinction between rural and urban was not as marked as might be supposed. The hills behind the cottage where Silas lived as a young child were wooded - across the valley would have been open fields and between Darshill and the town centre of Shepton less than a mile away would have been meadows and several farms. In many ways the situation could be said to anticipate the central thrust of Silas's working life, the connection between the town and the rural communities that surrounded it.

Silas and Shepton 1871 onwards

A frustration of studying history is that sometimes you just can't find the information which you know must be there. An example of this is the Davis family appearing to be totally missing from the 1861 census. My wife Christine has been through the Shepton Mallet Census line by line, including the Workhouse, and has used index searches for elsewhere in the country but with no success. Silas should be an easy name to spot so it would appear that they had somehow been missed. It has to be said that having failed when searching for other names in Shepton in the 1861 census that questions could be asked about its completeness.

Research by Christine Marshman has revealed that John Davis, Silas's father, had died in March 1859 aged 67 of asthma. The informant was his wife Mary Ann and at that time the family were still living in Darshill. The death of one of Silas's sisters, Martha Frances, of 'fits' (possibly epilepsy) at the age of 21 in April 1864 shows that by then the family were living in Cowl Street. Her mother Mary Ann is given as being present at the sad death.

In 1871 we can again locate the family living in the heart of town in Cowl Street.

Mary A Davis	head	widow	62	former velvet weaver	born Shepton Mallet
Ann Dixon	dau	married	35	wife velvet weaver	born Shepton Mallet
Mary Davis	dau	unmarried	32	velvet weaver	born Shepton Mallet
Albert Davis	son	unmarried	19	bread baker	born Shepton Mallet
Mary A Dixon	grandau		4	scholar	born Shepton Mallet

Mary Ann was by then a widow living at home with three of her children - a youngest son of 19 and two elder daughters, one an unmarried spinster of 32 and another married but living at home with a young child. Ann had married a Jacob Dixon but we have been unable to locate him in the census. The family is still involved with the velvet weaving trade but it is noticeable that the son has gone into something else - a sign of the decline in relative importance of the textile trade in Shepton Mallet.

Silas although only 22 has already left home and with his own family of a wife and two children was living in Town Street.

| Silas Davis | head | married | 22 | Postman | born Shepton Mallet |

Ann	wife	married	23	Postman's wife born Stoke Lane
William E	son		2	born Shepton Mallet
Emily	dau		under 1 month	born Shepton Mallet

It will be noted that Silas was already working for the Post Office. A trip to the archive room at the Post Office museum in London revealed some interesting information. Silas first joined the Post Office as a Temporary Rural Messenger on the 8 August 1869. His service as a civil servant started from the 4 November 1869 and the records show that from the 6 November 1869 he was a 'Rural Messenger - afterwards styled Rural Postman.' An appointment to the Post Office was of respectable significance, postmen being civil servants employed by the government.

His wages from when he started were fifteen shillings a week and for those of us used to annual increases it is a bit of a shock to discover that his basic wage did not increase until 1891! Even then it only went up a shilling. However it would appear that there were other allowances including good conduct stripes which helped to build up his wage.

It can be seen that his wife Ann was born in Stoke Lane - as Stoke St Michael was called before the Second World War. It must have been quite a strange decision to change the name of a village. Civil Registration records show that Silas Davis of Shepton Mallet and Anne Gregory of Stoke Lane had been married in the March quarter of 1868 three years before in Shepton Mallet.

Investigation back through the censuses reveals a little about her background.

1851   Stoke Lane Mendip

Ameriah Gregory	head	34	Maltster	Born Stoke Lane
Ann	wife	32	Knitter	Born Stoke Lane
Elizabeth	dau	10		Born Stoke Lane
Martha	dau	8		Born Stoke Lane
Ann	dau	3		Born Stoke Lane
Teresa	dau	11 month		Born Stoke Lane

Presumably Ameriah worked at the big maltings in Oakhill only a couple of miles walk down the lane. It is probable that his wife, also Ann, as a knitter was an outworker who worked at home whilst bringing up her young daughters.

In the1861 census thirteen year old Ann was not so easy to find, she was not in Stoke Lane. She was located in Shepton Mallet in the High Street household of Charles Goodenough, a confectioner and baker. It was not unusual for the better off traders of those days to be employing a young girl as a domestic servant although this would be definitely the lower end of domestic service as a career.

Ann Gregory   serv   13   Servant   Born Stoke Lane

Silas and Ann married on 26 January 1868 at the Independent Chapel in Shepton Mallet. Their marriage certificate shows that they were both aged 20. Silas was at that time listed as being a labourer and Ann a silk worker. It is interesting to note that Silas could write and signed his name whilst Ann marked her name with an X. It is also intriguing to see that at the time of the marriage in the Independent Chapel, Shepton Mallet, Ann's father Amariah gives his job as a 'beehive maker'.

By 1881 the family had grown considerably and were living in Cowl Street.

Silas Davis	head	32	Post messenger	Born Shepton Mallet
Ann	wife	33		Born Stoke Lane
William E	son	12	Errand Boy	Born Shepton Mallet
Emily J	daughter	10	Scholar	Born Shepton Mallet
Annie L	daughter	7	Scholar	Born Shepton Mallet
Alice R	daughter	4		Born Shepton Mallet
John A	son	4 months		Born Shepton Mallet

Research into the family history by Christine Marshman has revealed that this was shortly after a time of tragedy for the family. Four month old John had been one of a pair of twins. His baby twin brother Albert had died in February of pneumonia aged three months. The death certificate was signed by BN Hyatt one of a well known dynasty of doctors in Shepton Mallet.

The 1891 census reveals one more child Ernest H. who was then aged 6 and had been born on the 1 June 1884. Ernest is important to this tale, as it is through him that our main connection to the present day comes. The family at that time was living at 33 Catsash. Due to road renaming and numbering it is possible that this was the same as 1 Crown Cottages where Silas spent the rest of his life.

How had Shepton Mallet evolved by the 1870s and 80s? As previously mentioned the census figures show that it was of a relatively static size; 5149 in 1871 and 5322 in 1881. An interesting statistic is given that there were one thousand one hundred and fifty five inhabited houses - an average of nearly five persons per household. Today it is likely that the average is well below three people per household. When we look at the small size of the surviving cottages in Garston Street or Cowl Street it can be seen that they must have had a very different way of living for the large families with shared bedrooms, crowded living rooms and

High Street Shepton Mallet in the 1860s (postcard Adrian Pearse)

little of the privacy that we consider so important today. The impression of working communities of the late Victorian era is that people would have been out of doors a lot more and have known their neighbours well, helping each other in times of trouble. The memories of the elderly Sheptonians today talk of the former community spirit of the people living in the various parts of Shepton.

Kelly's Directory for 1875 paints quite a lively picture:

'Shepton Mallet is a manufacturing and market and union town, polling place for the Mid Somerset Division of the county, having two railway stations, one on the East Somerset line and the other on the Somerset and Dorset extension railway....

.... It is lighted with gas and well supplied with water. Within the last few years the paving and walks have been improved; many alterations have been carried out in the principle streets, and several handsome buildings have been erected.'

Silas's children would almost certainly have gone to the National School described by Kelly's as:

'The National School for boys, girls and infants is in the New Road (Waterloo Road): the buildings in which it is held was erected by subscription, aided by a grant from the Committee of Council on Education, in 1862, and is remarkably commodious and well ventilated.'

These buildings became the Senior School when the new infant school was built in 1906 and in the 1970s were converted to old people's flats.

Of the industry of Shepton Mallet, Kelly's reports the past extent of the woollen industry and the problems of earlier in the century before going on to observe,

'At the present time there is an important manufacture carried on in silk, velvet and crepe in which many hundred hands are constantly employed. There are several extensive breweries; Charlton Brewery and the Old Town Brewery are well known in this and the adjoining counties, and at the hamlet of Oakhill there is a brewery (established 1767); the whole are carried on with great success, and the locality has become celebrated for its ale and porter. Messrs Cox and Norseworthy confine themselves to brewing a fine light ale suitable for export to the East and West Indies; the brewery is near the centre of the town, and covers a large extent of ground….. Rope making and brick and tile making are carried on in the parish; there is also an extensive bacon-curing establishment at Darshill.'

Although there was still a considerable amount of textile industry there had been a decided shift to an emphasis on brewing. It should not be forgotten that Shepton was also a busy market town, an active centre for the farmers and the rural villages around it. A look through the entries in the directory reveals that the town had the following establishments and officers: a cemetery, a police station: a courthouse for petty sessions, the prison: an Inland Revenue office; a Duchy of Cornwall office; a public weighbridge; a district hospital; a stamp office; a post & money & telegraph order office; a gas works; a water company; a highways board and Turnpike company; two coroners; a registrar of births and deaths and a registrar of marriages; a newspaper; a Church; a Roman Catholic Church; four chapels of other denomination; a grammar school and two national schools and the two railways.

A look at the huge number of trades carried out in the town, from butchers and bakers to furriers, coopers, and tinplate workers makes you weep when you think of our depleted town centre today.

An analysis of the entries in the 1875 Kelly's directory reveals the following:

Shops: general shopkeepers 11, green grocers 3, marine stores 2, butchers etc 9, bakers confectioners etc 7, ironmongers 3, furniture 1, general/ linen draper 8, chemists 4, stationers 2, grocers 7, toy dealers 1, pianoforte warehouse 1, fishmonger 1, pawnbroker 1.

Professionals: accountant 2, vet 1, solicitor 3, auctioneer 2, surgeons / physicians 6.

Crafts and trades: boot and shoemakers 14, coal dealers 7, brick and tile maker 1, furrier 1, umbrella maker 1, glovemaker 1, saddler 3, dressmaker 7, printer 3, basket maker 3, photographer 1, tailor 6, builder 5, carpenter 4, gunmaker 1, plumber 1, whitesmith 1, hairdresser 4, timber dealer 1 salt merchant 1, watch and clockmakers 4, coachbuilder 2, cork cutter 1, plasterer 4, blacksmith 5, decorator 3, wheelwright 2, twine and ropemaker 1, cooper 2, milliner / straw hat maker 4, tin plate makers 4, stone and marble mason 1, cabinet maker 1, carrier 2, chimney sweeps 2.

Agriculture: farmers 25, cheese and corn factor 2, miller 2, dairyman 1, bone miller 1, manure manufacturer 1, seedsman 1, market gardener 1.

Pubs or beer sellers 31, brewers 6!

In the time Silas had his young family Shepton Mallet was certainly a lively town. There was very little that anyone needed that would not have been obtainable in the town and most things would even have been made locally.

Market square in the 1860's -pre drinking fountain (postcard Adrian Pearse)

The Post Office and the Royal Mail

The forty years during which Silas was treading his round was a period of remarkable evolution and growth both in scale and scope of services for the Post Office and Royal Mail. This brief overview has been drawn from a number of sources but particular reference has to be made to 'Shepton Mallet - An Historical and Postal Survey' by Eric H. Ford which was self published in a limited edition of 200 by the author in 1958. This is a most unusual local history book, giving a brief history of Shepton Mallet, a rather esoteric history of the post office nationally and locally and a fixation with postal franking stamps. However it does provide some information pertinent to this story.

At the current time it seems inevitable that the postal services in this country are about to be de-regulated and opened up to competition from other companies. Along with every other public service where competition has been introduced there will be the inevitable decline in service and increase in cost for the ordinary man in the street and the likelihood that within a few years the profits from the business will be creamed off to overseas companies. Why we have been inflicting these masochistic economic polices on ourselves for the best part of a generation is a mystery. The Royal Mail and Post Office has been the last to survive and there are good historical reasons for this. State control and monopoly of the Royal Mail was nothing to do with post war labour nationalizations but dates back nearly 400 years to when in 1635 Charles I opened up the Royal Posts to the use of the public. From 1657 an Act of Parliament fixed rates for sending letters throughout the Kingdom.

In these early days, the sending of mail was a very much a minority activity and the rates were not cheap - neither was the service that quick. A target of getting 95% of first class post delivered the next day was definitely not on the cards! A network of Postmasters gradually evolved, at first situated in local inns where the Innkeeper / Postmaster would collect mail from locals and take the deliveries of mail arriving. The associations with inns came largely through the use of horses and later mail coaches where the post boys would need to change or refresh their horse on long journeys. Locally The Old Down Inn at Emborough five miles north as Shepton Mallet was for a long time identified as an important post inn as the pub sign until recently recorded. There is an excellent section on the history of the Old Down Inn in 'Old Mendip' by Robin Atthill published in 1964.

By the early nineteenth century the postal service had grown in scale and most towns would have had Postmasters. Often these would have been shopkeepers with the post as a section of their business using their own staff and servants to effect local deliveries of letters. The novels of Jane Austin show the extensive use of letters by the upper middle classes at this time. Although many of her own letters to her family were destroyed enough remain to show that people of these classes were staying in touch with copious numbers of letters.

The Royal Mail moved up a gear in 1840. It was on January 10th that a social reformer Rowland Hill invented and introduced the 'Penny Black' the world's first and, without doubt most famous, postage stamp based on the simple idea of preprinting small pieces of paper which could be sold to be stuck on envelopes to show that postage had been paid, and then franked to demonstrate that it had been used. This led to a rapid expansion in the amount of post that was being sent. Locally Eric Ford quotes some very interesting figures. A survey for one week in 1838 before the introduction of the 'Penny Black' shows a total of 413 pieces of mail (excluding 70 newspapers) passing through the Shepton Mallet Post Office for all destinations. He points out that this was a relatively small number of items and suggests that the cost of sending letters could have restricted it: 4d to Wells, 5d to Bath and 6d to Taunton. By 1844, four years after the introduction of the 'Penny Black,' over 250 letters per week were being sent from Shepton Mallet to the villages of Evercreech, Batcombe and Stoney Stratton alone.

The reduction of the cost of postage had the effect of ending the element of private competition to the state monopoly of mail that had existed until then. Carriers of parcels etc had often been able to offer to deliver mail - if disguised as a packet or parcel. However the reduction of price to 1d made this uneconomic - a situation that has continued to this day.

The huge increase in the quantity of mail and the requirement to sell stamps led to the need for separate post office counters which resulted in the network of sub post offices within other shops that we can still recognize today - and regret its ongoing rapid dismantling. The Post Office was also extending its range of services at this time. In 1838 Money Order Offices were formalized where customers were provided with a secure means of sending small amounts of money to people in other parts of the country. An order could be purchased at one office, sent to a recipient who could then take it to an office near them to cash. A development of this, the Postal Order that we know today, was introduced in 1881. In 1841 the system of Registered Mail was introduced and then in 1846 the scheme still in operation for the delivering of newspapers and other printed matter in special covers at a reduced rate was introduced.

1861 saw the introduction of the Post Office Savings Bank - pre-runner of today's Girobank. This introduced saving facilities, perhaps for the first time for many, to the ordinary working man. Within two years 2,500 post offices operated the savings bank and it was soon estimated that there were three and a half million savings accounts open - a true social revolution which perhaps says more about Victorians than many other indicators.

Twenty year old Silas joined the Post Office in 1869 which was a momentous year for the Post Office in Shepton Mallet. It was the year that the Postmaster of two years' standing moved into a shop on the corner of Commercial Road and the High Street which is currently occupied by the Brittannia building society. Prior to that it is difficult to pin-point where the Post Office had been located. It would appear to have been in various locations in the High Street or Market Place depending on who was Postmaster.

1869 was also the year when the telegraph service was authorized for Shepton Mallet along with 22 other towns in the West Country (although it probably took a couple of years to get up and running.) It is from then that telegram boys were employed to deliver their messages, good or often bad.

Kelly's Directory of 1875 lists under official establishments for the town:-

'Post & Money Order & Telegraph Office, Savings Bank & Government Annuity & Insurance Office, High Street. Postmaster Charles William Fudge.
     Letters dispatched to London & towns in Eastern and Southern Counties at 1pm; Wells 12.50pm & to Bath, Bristol, Ireland, Scotland & the North can be posted until 1.45pm; to South Wales 4.15pm.
     London and all parts, until 8pm; with additional stamp, until 8.25pm; & can be registered here until 7.30 & and with an additional 4d until 8pm.
     Letters delivered from London & all parts at 7am and 2.40pm. On Sundays there is only one delivery, commencing at 7 - 10 am only.
     Money orders issued and paid, also Post Office Savings Bank and Government Annuity and Insurance business transacted from 10 till 6 and on Saturdays from 10 till 8pm.'

The personal entry for the postmaster shows:-

'Fudge Charles William, chemist, grocer, & post office, High Street.'

It can be seen that by the time Silas started at the Post Office it was already a well-organised and sophisticated organization with high standards of service in operation. In fact it appears a more comprehensive service than we have today. There are now no Sunday deliveries and if you took a postal order along for cashing at 7.30pm on a Saturday I don't think you would get much joy.

Until the mid 1870s horse or horse and carriage from Bath, it would seem, brought in the majority of the post. The legendary horse-drawn mail coaches out of London had died out in the 1850s as soon as the railways replaced them. Although there was a railway line via Westbury from the 1850s it appears that it was not until the Somerset and Dorset Railway was extended to Bath in the mid 1870s that rail took over as the main way of delivering the post sacks to Shepton Mallet.

The Postmaster changed in 1880 when Frederick Coombs took over at the same premises. He is described in the 1883 edition of Kelly's Directory as

'Post Office, tea dealer, provisions merchant, genuine drug and patent medicine, warehouse and manufacture of horse and cattle condiment.'

An even wider ranging business than his predecessor - but at least now the Postmaster role is reported first. We have already seen that in the census of 1881 Silas was listed as being a Post Messenger. He was still one of very few. Frederick Coombs is recorded as 'Postmaster and Grocer employing 3 men, 2 boys and 5 women,' presumably to cover his whole business. One employee, John Hatcher aged 21, a Post Office Assistant / Clerk was lodging with him.

During Silas's time the number of staff increased considerably. A photo of the Post Office staff in Fred Davis's book 'Shepton Mallet Camera' taken after 1900

Shepton Mallet Post Office staff, probably after the 1904 expansion.
Silas is fourth from left in the middle row. (photo Christine Marshman)

shows 31 Post Office staff. Throughout Silas's time with the Post Office it continued to develop, both locally and nationally. In 1883 the parcel post was introduced, using the same service for the delivery of parcels. In the mid 1880s it was reported that there were more civil servants employed in the Post Office than in any other government department. By the time Silas retired in 1908 the next major development was on the horizon with the introduction of the revolutionary old age pensions in 1909 which until recent years were primarily paid through the Post Office.

The quantity of post that was delivered continued to grow as an almost inevitable part of the social changes of the last third of the nineteenth century. The population of the country as a whole continued to grow apace. Following the introduction of compulsory education in the 1870s it was also a much more educated population with a far greater proportion of the working classes able to read and write. It was also a much more mobile population. Looking at parish registers prior to this period it is noticeable that it was only the upper classes and the tradesman class who tended to move more than a few parishes away from their place of birth. However in the last quarter of the nineteenth century there is more evidence for young adults from the countryside moving to the towns with girls like Silas's wife Ann becoming servants in the local town. Some young men, unable to see a future in farm labouring moved to London or even emigrated. Some of the figures for this may have been exaggerated and examination of the census also shows some returning - however there is no doubt that a lot more people were moving about, away from their families but with a will to stay in touch through letters.

It should also be remembered that this was a period when although some historians focus on continued poverty the reality of society was of rising standards of living. There was also increasing leisure time, particularly for a rising number of middle class women - renowned for their letter writing. Christmas cards, Valentine cards and birthday cards were also becoming increasingly fashionable which all added to a substantial increase in the amount of post.

Things were also developing in Shepton Mallet. In 1881 the authorities gladdened the hearts of all postmen by decreeing that all properties should be named or numbered. Prior to this addresses such as 'Mr C Brown, Shepton Mallet' must have led to a scratching of the head in a town of 5,500 people.

By the mid 1880s the volume of work passing through made it necessary for the opening of a dedicated Post Office - this was opened in 1885 a few doors up the High Street where Martins the newsagents is now situated. It stayed here for the rest of the time Silas was working there, not moving to the grand Market Square

Post Office clock jutting out over the high street in the early 1900s
(postcard Janet Moore)

premises, from where the sorting office still operates, until as late as 1925.

The site of the 1885 Post Office can be easily spotted from the 'Post Office clock' which still projects into the street from above the shop and still provides time for the High Street - usually reasonably correctly as well. Eric Ford reports at some length that apparently this never actually was a Post Office clock:-

"A well known firm of stationers and printers (almost certainly A Byrt whose premises were between the corner shop and the Post Office and were publishers of the Shepton Mallet Journal) who owned a clock suitable for public use agreed to have it erected outside premises in the High Street that were tenanted by the Postmaster and used as the Post Office. They also agreed that when the clock had been erected, they would formally hand it over to the Local Board (the forerunner of the Shepton Mallet Urban District Council which was set up a few years later).

   The Postmaster agreed 'to daily wind and keep wound the said clock and keep Greenwich time free of all charges therefore'

   The Local Board agreed 'to pay for repairs so long as the Public Auditor shall pass the charges"

Eric Ford also comments on the detail which is available in the records of the Post Office. An illustration he cites is almost certainly directly relevant to Silas. He records that in 1886 there was a decision passed by the Post Master General that a lamp be provided for the Shepton Mallet - Wraxall Green rural postman to enable him to read addresses on letters when delivering in the dark. In the days when there were certainly no streetlights in rural areas and no handy pocket torches it can be imagined that this was a badly-needed accessory for Silas as he struggled to identify which letter went where on his massive round at either end of the short dark winter days.

By 1891 the postal work in and out of Shepton had grown to such an extent that the Post Master General decided that future appointments of postmaster would be at his discretion - basically this meant that they then became full time professionally trained members of the Postal Services - rather than the mixed occupation shop keepers they had been up to then. The first of these was AA Taylor appointed in 1897 who was succeeded by J. Longstaffe in 1899 and G Gould in 1903. Mr Gould was Postmaster until 1916 and spoke at Silas's retirement presentation in 1908.

The development of the Shepton Mallet Post Office continued and in 1904 an additional 33 sub post offices were transferred to the town for administration from the Bath office. This formed the basis for the postal sorting district of today serving many parishes to the south and south east of the town.

Silas's round - a reconstruction

And so I start my reconstruction attempt, to work out the route which Silas would have followed. It is Christmas Eve 2005, has just gone eight o'clock in the morning and is still half dark with grey skies - in this light truly warranting the description of leaden. The hills to the north, grey green, standing steeply over the town. Silas would have left his small cottage down near the Crown Inn at the bottom of Cowl Street and walked up Tipcote Hill and Town Street through the Market Place and along to the Post Office. For most of the time he was delivering this would have been in what is now the southern half of Martins - beneath where the Post Office clock still hangs out over the High Street giving the time to the town centre.

By 1900 the sending of Christmas cards would have been well established - and those people who could not get home to their families would have also been sending letters. Posting early for Christmas had probably not been thought of and there is little doubt that Christmas Eve would have been one of Silas's heaviest deliveries of the year - though of course he would also be going out again tomorrow to do the delivery on Christmas Day.

The Post Office must have been a lively bustle in the early morning on Christmas Eve. Once the arriving mail had been bought from both stations it would be sorted into the various rounds. The sorting office in the centre of town now still has the increased activity as Christmas approaches. When I go to fetch the post for work I see the numerous postal staff sorting the post into the various rounds - the pigeonholes still separated 'rural' and 'town'. Today most of it is then loaded into the long row of small red post office vans that queue along Great Ostry awaiting their turn to be loaded.

Walking up the High Street I realize that nearly all the buildings I pass would have been familiar to Silas. Most of the shop fronts have changed, as have the uses of the buildings but the actual street today would have been instantly recognizable to Silas. When you look above street level you can see the mixture of shops, grander houses and cottages that it would have been. Some of the grander houses are now solicitors offices or converted into flats. A few of the cottages, which at one time would have been small shops, have returned to uses as cottages as the High Street slowly reverts to the more mixed usage of retail, commercial and residential that would have been typical of the nineteenth century.

I suspect that in Victorian times there would have been a bit more activity at this time of a morning - however people are around and getting ready for the day. In the newsagent customers are coming in for their papers and cigarettes, the rounds are all marked up and waiting for the paperboys who take advantage of the holidays to deliver later than when they are at school.

From the bakers across the road is the gorgeous smell of baking bread. Inside the shop they are already stacking the fresh loaves on the shelves behind the counter and placing buns in the window. There are so few of these local tradesmen now compared to those that Silas would have seen. As I pass up the High Street I notice the saucy lingerie shop with mannequins modeling some extremely scant purple underwear - somehow I am sure Silas would never have experienced this sight window-shopping in Victorian Shepton!

As Silas, carrying his sack at its heaviest, passed Townsend he would have walked up the embankment built in the 1850s to take him over the railway line. The post and rails on the right hand side Chris Challis informs me are original railway railings. First on the right would have been the cricket ground - long since converted into extended gardens for Summerleaze house, then an army camp, then the Clark's shoe factory and now about to metamorphise once again into a Tesco's super store. You can still see the railway station down below; now the home of a cleaning equipment wholesaler. Silas would have been a boy when the railway first arrived in town with great celebrations. For the first few years Shepton was the terminus of the line, which headed eastward to Westbury and then on to London. However after a few years it was extended to Wells and beyond.

We have become so accustomed to it that you usually forget you are rising up an embankment. However once past the 1970s Mendip District Council offices on your left you can look down from the old bridge into the unfilled cutting below and see just how high above the natural level you have climbed.

Here I am faced with a choice as to which way Silas would have gone. By car today the natural way is out via Cannards Grave via the main road and two round-abouts before turning right back to Beardly Batch. However a glance at the map suggests that on foot there is a more direct way up Compton Road. I am sure Silas would not have walked an unnecessarily long route so I am taking the route straight up Compton Road. This would have looked very different in Silas's day. Only the first few houses on either side would have been built, and these probably towards the end of the time that Silas was covering this route. Most of the houses - especially higher up the road are definitely from the inter-war period when judging from their size this was a road where the better off tradesmen of Shepton would have built their houses. To the right is the entry to the huge Ridgeway estate. A council development dating from after the Second World War and the need to build 'homes fit for heroes'.

As I pass Middleton House, Compton Road narrows and becomes what it always would have been, a narrow country lane providing access to the fields on either side. Although not quite at the top yet it has been quite a pull up, not as steep as the hills on the north side of the town but looking back in the early morning haze it is interesting to note that the main part of the town has already disappeared - lost from view in its valley.

It is interesting to speculate where Silas started his round. We know from the newspaper reports that he covered Pylle but did he deliver any post before he got there? Perhaps he delivered to Cannards Grave - quite a sizable hamlet on the Fosse Way with two Inns, at least two farms and a number of cottages. It even had a small church built during the time Silas was covering his round. If he did come out by this Compton Road route surely he covered the farms and cottages in East Compton and I would imagine it is almost certain that he would have delivered to Beard Hill Farm and the cottages there on the ridge before dropping down to Pylle.

As we crest the top of the rise, the landscape stretches out around us with Whitstone hill away to the right. The fields are relatively small around here with plenty of trees in the hedgerows - trees would be encouraged in the hedgerows, an important source of timber. There is a group of store cattle in a field to the right. In Silas's time more of the fields would have had small herds of mixed coloured shorthorn cattle - providing milk for the dairies in the town. Alan Hoskins, an elderly retired farmer, told me a few years ago that up to the Second World War there were nineteen dairies in Shepton Mallet.

The trees stand bare with their gaunt frameworks exposed to the chill morning air. Silas would have seen the trees at all seasons, clothed in the bright greens of spring, their summer maturity and the many autumn shades of brown. Over to the right is another gaunt framework against the skyline - but this is something Silas definitely would not have seen - a mobile phone mast. I also now notice the telegraph poles carrying their phone wires - would Silas have seen these. I doubt it. Although the telegraph service was introduced in the 1880s and there may have been telegraph posts along the railways and main roads, the spread of telephones wires to private houses was definitely a twentieth century development in technology. The phone mast is probably a sign that the need for these will soon also pass.

I can hear the raucous cries of some rooks in some trees across the fields but note in the recently dunged field a flock of seagulls. Is this something Silas would have seen? When I was young I was told gulls only came inland when there was stormy weather at sea but they now appear permanent visitors - in fact you don't seem to see that many more at the coast.

Over the crest of the plateau now and the countryside opens out still more. Even on this dull morning I can see in the distance the hill behind Pylle that I am making my way towards a couple of miles ahead. Only a couple of minutes away in a car as I would normally travel. How long will it take me to get there this morning? I walk at a reasonably brisk pace - you can tell by my panting and the sweat on my brow. I knew I should not have put on such a thick jumper this morning.

But how did Silas walk? From his picture he looks to have been a slim wiry chap full of energy. I imagine carrying his bag he would have made his way with an energetic firm busy stride, bustling along at a good pace. When you know that he retired early you wonder if it was the constant wear on his body which so much walking had entailed had literally worn bits of him out. He would have had to take care what he wore depending on the seasons. His Postman's uniform and cap would have been compulsory. He would have needed his weatherproof cape - did he roll this up and put in his sack when he wasn't wearing it. I am doing this on a relatively mild day (for December) with no rain or wind - on many days Silas would not have been so lucky. In his forty years he would have had to tolerate all conditions from driving snow to blistering heat.

The warm smell of horse dung reaches me and I spot some lumps dropped in the road which have been squashed by a passing motor car. Of course this would have been a very familiar smell to Silas with virtually all the traffic on the road in his day being horse drawn. In fact the smell would have been so familiar I doubt if he would even have noticed it.

A group of long tailed tits fly across me into the hedgerow and I note that here what was once a hedge has outgrown itself into a scrubby row of 'trees'. These will never amount to much - they will not become the fine timber trees that we see in so many hedgerows. This hedge has probably not even seen the barbarous flails of a tractor mounted hedge-cutter for ten years, however in Silas's times at this season the farm workers - especially the elderly - would be employed at hedging. Properly cutting and laying the hedges and trimming the new growth. Clearing out the ditches as they went and lighting bonfires to burn up the cuttings. I remember an old hedger telling me of the independence of this job where you were left to get on with it for weeks at a time. On any particular day able to choose which side of the hedge you cut so you could avoid being exposed to the worst of the weather.

Ahead of me now are the farms and cottages of East Compton spread out in an uneven row running from left to right. A couple of hundred yards beyond them up a slight rise runs the road from Glastonbury and Pilton - allegedly along an old ridgeway route which the romantics have suggested had ceremonial significance in early Christian times. Not at all sure about that but it does intrigue me that the entire settlement of East Compton is set back from this road.

It is also here that Compton Road / Lane, which I have followed from Shepton Mallet, now becomes a no through road. There is a footpath shown on the map that joins the Glastonbury road. I hope I can find it otherwise I will have to cut through the yard of cider-making farmer Roy Trott and I can see his cows are in there at the moment, being milked.

Interesting - the road is clearly still there running straight ahead for only a couple of hundred yards to the Glastonbury road. It is however now a well made up private driveway and to my left I pass a charming little gentleman's country residence that looks straight out of the pages of Jane Austin. Presumably at some time the through road was incorporated into the 'park' and the public discouraged.

There is a footpath sign opposite pointing the way over the fields to Beard Hill 1 mile away - though I think this would be quite a short mile. However it being rather wet under foot and not really wanting to struggle through fields I turn left along the main road looking for another track which is shown on the map cutting through to Beard Hill.

As I walk along this stretch of main road I pass a cider orchard - not a traditional one by the looks of it but it is a reminder that back along the road in West Pennard you would have been right in one of the main traditional cider apple growing areas of Somerset with the soil said to be especially favourable to the fruit. In a dunged field to the left is a large flock of starlings who rise as a mass and deposit themselves on the telephone wires and surrounding trees.

The track to the right runs between two hedges and is obviously still used, at least occasionally, by tractors. There are signs that at some point it had a firm stone surface but for the main part now it has a high ridge of grass in the middle with ruts on either side. Tracks like this were obviously once country lanes just like many others but never of sufficient importance to be taken in hand by the council and tarmaced. I suspect however that this one may have had stone surfacing in Silas's day.

I walk past a small holly tree which is nice on Christmas Eve. There is not a lot of holly in the hedges around here - presumably it was never planted and has found its way in through naturalisation. At first glance I think this is one of those holly trees that does not have berries but then I notice a solitary red spot - presumably the birds have already had their fill of any others.

The constant drone of traffic has receded into the background here and I hear the blackbirds singing strongly - in the distance I can hear a cow which for some unknown reason has decided to moo loudly and repeatedly. The field to my right is bare apart from the stumps of a crop of forage maize that has been harvested during the autumn. This is not a crop that Silas would have been familiar with in the fields of the Victorian era.

The track has emerged into Platterwell Lane - a lane that can only just have qualified to have been taken on by the county. It is extremely narrow and in parts has grass in the middle running over a mile from Beard Hill to the east of Pilton. I am only walking the short part of it to Beard Hill Farm which I can see ahead on the other side of the A37. From this angle I have a good view of the fine set of Victorian farm buildings, which I normally flash past without a glance as I drive along the main road.

Just before I emerge onto the A37 on my left is a row of four cottages in a terrace, two very small and two larger. Presumably these were for farm workers of different grades - or perhaps family size. On the right hand side of the lane each cottage has what would originally have been an allotment - though these have now been converted into extensions to their gardens.

I have taken refuge from the fast traffic on the A37 in the entrance to Platterwell Farm (where does that name come from?) Ahead of me the Roman Fosseway stretches straight across the valley about a mile before rising up Pye Hill over the Pennard ridge. On the other side of the road I have just passed, almost invisible, three massive stone arches built into the hillside, the remnants of limekilns. I have been passing these regularly for nearly thirty years and I had only thought there were two. In Silas's time lime burning was an important rural industry to provide the lime to sweeten the pastures and encourage grass growth. The 1881 census shows a lime burner living in the nearest part of Pylle but whether he worked here or in the big Lime Works by the railway on the other side of Pylle I have not been able to find.

As I dodge traffic walking along the grass verge there are horses in neatly laid out paddocks to my right. Each horse is wearing a canvas protective jacket. I wonder if in Silas's days the horses would have been wearing jackets - not sure. In those days the horses were economically very important; would they have been out in the fields at all? Those belonging to the gentry would undoubtedly have had stables and grooms to look after them. In Pylle the census shows a number of carters who would surely also have kept their horses in stables as a norm - allowing them out in the fields maybe when they were not being used - but surely not at this time of year. Today's often over fed pampered pet horses probably need to be in the fields to work off their energy but maybe those of Silas's time got worked enough not to need to be left looking lonely, cold and damp, trapped in paddocks delineated by electric strip fences.

Just passing Dukes Farm - the first house from Silas's time that definitely counts as Pylle. It is a very interesting building this one. The mullioned windows on the front suggest it should be of some antiquity but other features are not so old. On the censuses I found it once as three cottages, once empty and once referred to as 'The Old Duke'. Perhaps in earlier days it was an inn - there must have been a number along the route of the Fosse. It was definitely not identified as a farm which seems to have been a 20th century metamorphosis - I will have to find out more.

I force myself to hang on to the hedge as more traffic roars past from both directions. Few drivers even seem to see me or acknowledge my presence - surely I am a better driver than that. I am sure Silas didn't have these problems though there would have been plenty of horse drawn trader's carts along such a major road. It always amazes me when I read old newspapers how often quite serious traffic accidents were reported in those days. Carts overturning, or getting entangled with each other, horses bolting, drivers drunk in charge. The miracle really seems to be that we have so few accidents these days given the amount of traffic - have we all developed some extra sensory power that by and large helps us avoid each other when hurtling around at 70 miles an hour in our tin boxes?

I often feel anxious for the postmen in their little red vans as they attempt to deliver along these roads. Pulling into drive entrances and the passing traffic seemingly oblivious to the requirement they have to open the door and get out. Then having to pull across the face of oncoming traffic to another driveway on the other side of the road. Constantly having to find a rare gap in the traffic to allow them to pull back out into the road. It can't be easy - perhaps Silas's round on foot does have something to say for it.

Past Willow Farm - quite a tall building which again wasn't a farm in Silas's day. Somewhere around here there was a chapel and there is something about this building that has made me wonder if this was it but now on closer inspection I am less sure. There are a few cottages here. It is still about half a mile from Street-on-the-Fosse (Pylle) and this area was always listed separately on the census - sometimes referred to as Hedge - I am about to turn right down Hedge Lane. I notice the number on one of the cottages - 866. No, there were never that many houses in Pylle, the numbers come from a numbering system of the Portman Estate which owned Pylle in the nineteenth century. This was an incredibly prosperous time for the Portman family and they had extensive properties right across the country. The numbering started at 1 in Cornwall and had reached the 2000's by the time they reached London.

Going down Hedge Lane and straight ahead of me is a clear view of one of Somerset's most prominent landmarks, the hump of Glastonbury Tor with its ruined church tower on top. You seem to spot this wherever you go around here and I am surprised I have not noticed it before this morning. It is about eight or nine miles ahead of me. Less than a mile to my left is the steep sided Pennard Ridge which seems from here to run nearly all the way to the Tor. In fact the prominence of the Tor comes not from its size but from its isolation, rising alone from the flat moors which are little above sea level.

Hedge Lane is a welcome relief from the roar of the traffic, though I do have to move to the side twice to allow cars to pass - but at least they acknowledge me with a slight wave. A man at the end of his drive says a friendly good morning and we comment on the mildness of the weather. He is checking his post box - an 'Alsatian lives here' sign on the gate - presumably the postman does not feel inclined to go to the front door.

At the end of the lane are the two Hedge Farms. Old Hedge Farm is down a drive across a field on from the end of the road. A very traditional looking old Somerset Farm. The newer Hedge Farm appears to be a late Victorian farm built very much in an estate style - presumably by the Portman Estate. The square solid lines and relatively wide flat roof are similar to a number across this region. Behind but now hidden are a fine set of Victorian model farm buildings which have now been converted to some very spacious and luxurious dwellings which fetch a high price.

I suspect Silas may have had a quiet curse to himself every time he had to deliver to Hedge Farm. It is a good half-mile along the lane and probably added around 20 minutes on to his walk. I check the time on my phone and notice that I have been going well over an hour. Silas would probably by now only have delivered a handful of letters. There is a footpath way marked across a few fields to Street-on-the-Fosse. Perhaps Silas would have taken this to cut off the corner. However it looks a bit boggy so I return to the Fosse by the way I have come.

Back to the roar of the traffic on the A37 but now with the luxury of a much welcomed pavement. Ahead to the left there is the flash of brake lights as cars slow to turn into Thorner's Farm Shop. This appears to be doing a roaring trade this morning as people come to collect their Christmas meat and turkeys. Thorner's is one of the new generation of farm shops. A few thousand square feet and well fitted-out selling a range of locally-produced foodstuffs and gift items as well as the butchers on which it is based. Over the past few years these farm shops have grown hugely to now be significant players in the retail market and there are signs that rather than copying the supermarkets the boot is one the other foot with supermarkets trying to mimic them with attempts to suggest they are selling wholesome local food. Long may the success and expansion of these farm shops continue as it provides at least a part of an answer to the survival of our traditional family farms in this country.

In Silas's time Street-on-the-Fosse had a butcher - who of course would have been very closely connected to local farmers. Christmas Eve must have been equally busy for him as the villagers (if such you can call them in this federation of hamlets) called to collect their Christmas joints, geese or the newly popular turkeys - for which, perhaps, prudent housewives had been putting a little bit of money away for a few months before. He may well have also had to get out his horse and cart to deliver to the larger houses scattered around the locality.

I pass a triangular milestone which informs me that I am now 3 miles from Shepton Mallet and 11 miles from Ilchester - fortunately I am not walking all that way. Apparently there is now a society dedicated to identifying and preserving milestones which have a habit of disappearing - even the old-fashioned white finger signposts are now rapidly becoming a thing of the past.

Into Street-on-the-Fosse proper now and there are quite a number of cottages along the west side of the road. I don't think you could ever have called them anything grander than cottages. Most of these would appear to have been here since Silas's time - but perhaps some of the red-bricked pairs could date from the twentieth century.

To the right, slightly down from the level of the road, is the site of the former Pylle railway station - the buildings still recognizable though converted to residential use. They are set down lower than the road and the railway ran beneath the raod which was lifted over a bridge to create sufficient headroom. When Silas first did his round this railway line would have been part of an attempt to run from Cardiff to Paris. A boat across the Bristol Channel, then train from Burnham-on-Sea to Poole then another boat. This was not a great success and in the 1870s just down the line at Evercreech Junction an ambitious extension was built to take the Somerset and Dorset line up over the Mendips to Bath. Pylle then became the first station on the branch line from Evercreech Junction to Burnham. However it appears to have remained an active station. Census records show a number of railway employees and farmers would have bought their milk, livestock and other produce to the station to go to town. Shepton shopkeeper Chris Challis was talking to an elderly person about an even more lonely station at Maesbury and was surprised to learn that around 19 farmers a day delivered their milk to the station.

I am now outside the Portman Arms, a very recently deceased pub. I saw a report in the local paper only a couple of weeks ago that the owner has applied for it to cease being a pub and turn it into a bed and breakfast with the buildings out the back used for holiday lets. As it hasn't appeared to be open the last couple of times I have driven past during an evening I assume it is now shut. It is a shame every time a pub shuts but we have to accept there have been social changes - particularly over the past 20 years - drinking at home seems to have become more the norm - the only pubs that survive are those that pander to the decadence of eating out.

It should also be remembered that in years gone by many pubs were not considered an economic unit in their own right. Often the innkeeper would have had another business or there would have been a smallholding attached. We know that this pub in Silas's time was run by William Moody who was also a surveyor and auctioneer - running repository sales from the yards to the rear of the pub. I doubt if the pub itself is that old. From its style I suspect that it was built by the Portman Estate deliberately to capitalize on the trade generated from the railway - accommodation for the commercial travellers who would have stayed whilst visiting the local farms. Perhaps this replaced the 'Old Duke' mentioned earlier?

I pass the petrol station with the yard for Smiths coaches adjoining. This is now one of very few petrol stations along the Fosseway between Shepton and Yeovil. When I first drove the road about 30 years ago there were perhaps a dozen. Following the closure of the two at Lydford within the past two years I think this may now be the only one. The rural petrol station is another dying trade - ironic when you look at the massive increase in traffic roaring past over the same period. I wonder if this garage may have been the site of the blacksmiths that was in Street-on-the-Fosse when Silas was delivering. I expect that would have been a place where he would often have paused to catch up on local gossip - or pass it on - with the farmers waiting to have their horses shod.

Now at the current Sub Post Office, come small village stores - yes this one has not yet closed as so many village shops have - a trend the current government seem so keen to hasten by ensuring pensions have to be paid direct into a bank. Perhaps the busy roadside location has ensured it an extended life. The ER on the front of the postbox confirms that this was not the original location of the Sub

The 'Post Office' Pylle. Photo from 1904 - probably soon after it had become the latest Post Office (postcard Adrian Pearse)

Post Office. A few cottages along is 'The Old Post Office' though in fact this would appear to have been one of a number. In Silas's time it seems to have moved with each census. Around 1900 it was round the corner into the lane to Pylle in the schoolhouse attached to the local school. The schoolmaster's wife was the Postmistress. Silas would have called here to drop off and collect some letters both in the morning on his way out and in the afternoon on his way back.

Nice little feature in the wall here - an alcove with a tap. Quite low down, the level of the road will have risen over the years. This may have been the source of water for local cottages or it could have been somewhere for passing horses to get a drink. The school itself has now been converted into a small village hall. It is an encouraging feature that so many small villages have active village halls enthusiastically run by volunteers. In towns there is often a problem with finding such community rooms - in Shepton Mallet there would be very few if it were not for the schools. On my left I can see a newly constructed car park showing that there is activity here. Mind you its main use in the year is as a base for traffic control for the Glastonbury Music Festival - a couple of miles away down the lane and over the fields.

Having turned down the lane to Pylle I realize that I have missed Pye Hill where the Fosseway rises up over the Pennard ridge and Writh Farm now across the fields to my left. I think it most probable that Silas did a sort of a figure of eight route and this would have been taken in on his way back. I can also see the wooded entrance to a very steep sided wooded valley which runs sharply into the ridge - something to explore some time.

To my right I can see on open expanse of fields gradually sloping upward back towards Beard Hill. Nearly all the fields are pasture, probably more would have been arable in Silas's time. I suspect some of the fields would have been smaller then but this is a view which Silas would recognize.

About half a mile ahead of me I can see the short tower of Pylle church. The 'village' of Pylle is much as it was over 100 years ago. Virtually nothing there then - as now. The Church, Pylle Manor with farm attached, two pairs of farm cottages, a grand rectory hidden away in the trees and perhaps one or two more houses. I suspect at some period slightly earlier than Silas a 'lord of the manor' had 'encouraged' the village to develop at Street-on-the-Fosse. From the census it is obvious that most of the workers on Pylle Manor Farm lived in the cottages at Street-on-the-Fosse.

Having been walking for approaching two hours and the road passing over a little tinkling stream my thoughts turn towards the possibility of 'taking a leak.' This must have been something that was very familiar to Silas. He probably had favourite spots on route where he knew he could slip into the trees or behind a hedge to gain the desirable amount of invisibility. I went out with a farm animal feed salesman of the old school one day. He knew which farms he would get a cup of tea at - indeed it seemed to be all of them. About mid morning he suggested that he had drunk enough tea and something else would be desirable - sure enough the next farm offered a glass of cider. Although motorized this salesman had similar needs and every now and then through the day he would cry out 'pee stop' and pull into a suitable field gateway he knew of.

Manor Farm in Silas's time was the bigger of two major farms in the parish at 800 acres, large even by today's standards locally. (Hedge Farm with 500 acres was the other). Today, although the buildings appear rather old fashioned it still appears to be a dairy farm, rather spilling out into the road. There is the marvelous sweet smell of well-fermented silage and a group of cattle eating in a yard. In Silas's day silage was unknown, grass would have been conserved as hay - which has a similarly pleasant if sometimes musty smell. There are some huge square hay bales in the yard each a meter high and at least two metres long. Two massive tractors pass, the first pulling a railed feeder in which one of these bales can be put and pulled to where the cattle feed. The second tractor, more of a teleporter, has a massive spike on the front for lifting the huge hay bales. In Silas's days the hay would have been cut out of ricks where it had been

The Church in Pylle.(postcard Adrian Pearse)

laid loose after drying and then forked into a horse drawn cart to be taken to feed the cattle. Same operation - different technology.

Past a very interesting pair of small estate bungalows- for want of a better term. I wonder whether these where for farm workers or for workers in Pylle Manor House which comes into view as I round the bend. This is a gaunt imposing residence, upright and grey - something of a French feel to it but with the farm buildings crowding up on its side. During Silas's time it was used as the farmhouse for farmer Cary who must have been a significant tenant farmer for the Portman Estate. In the first half of the twentieth century this was the home of Archie Garton a well known local character; a member of the family which had owned the Anglo Brewery in Shepton Mallet as well as others around the country. Archie was a military man in both world wars, a prominent councillor on the Rural District Council, a well known speaker of and writer on the local dialect. He was also a promoter of crafts and wrought iron work in particular. There is evidence of this on the gates to the Manor and around the little church. Above the church gate is a crafted crest with three crows or ravens - I will have to find out whose crest this is.

Just past the manor is a large pond - it appears to be ornamental, dammed by the road and an outlet running underneath to a slight drop the other side where a stream recommences. Ponds of course were a lot more common in Silas's time, particularly for providing cattle, sheep and horses with somewhere to drink.

Oh a flash of colour - a kingfisher darts away towards the trees at the far side of the pond but I get a clear view to confirm its identity. On Christmas Eve my first kingfisher of the year, despite taking my elder son bird watching fairly regularly.

Here there is an older cider orchard with the trees now bare apart from their garlands of mistletoe - a nice seasonal touch. In Silas's time many farms would have made their own cider and although it became illegal to give it as part of a labourer's wages it would still have been an expected perk especially at harvest time.

The road splits two ways here. To the right is the lane to Pilton. Silas may well have had a detour here to the Lime Works a few hundred yards along beside the railway line. From the old Ordnance Survey maps this appears to have been quite extensive but when I went to look for remains there was very little to be seen so I won't repeat that today. Instead I turn to the left as the narrow lane climbs up the steep Pennard ridge. To my right higher up and hidden is the rectory - an imposing building for so small a parish - probably because at the start of Silas's time the incumbent would appear to have been a member of the Portman family. Becoming a clergyman was still considered a good occupation for younger sons who had little prospect of inheriting a significant part of the estate.

Got to stop to take a breather - I suspect that sharp climb up from Pylle to Little Pennard where I am now may even have made Silas catch his breath. The lane rose through almost a cutting with a profusion of ferns growing on the damp banks on either side, drifts of dry leaves, mainly oak and beech, beside the road where they have been dropped in drifts by the wind which must fairly howl up this gully.

At the top the fields have opened out on either side again, the crest of Creech Hill away to the left. Little Pennard is a collection of a few cottages and a largish looking farm. I would assume that Silas would have made his deliveries here before turning right down towards East Pennard.

The lane slopes down towards East Pennard and already there is a subtle change in the landscape. In Silas's time Pennard House was the seat of the Napier family and the large beech trees in the fields here give an almost park like feel - although it is still working farm land. To my left though is a small paddock with a few bent old cider apple trees with huge bunches of mistletoe. A little wren just crosses the road in front of me seeking better business in one hedge than the other.

I can hear the barking of a pack of hounds - presumably the hunt is out over the hill down beyond Wraxall - you sometimes see the horse boxes along the verges of the A37 where you drive towards Yeovil. I can still hear the hounds and think I hear a huntsman's horn. I didn't know hunt the was out on Christmas Eve - their big meet is on Boxing Day from Castle Cary. Presumably this would be the Sparkford and Blackmore Vale Hunt. Of course this is the year that hunting with dogs has been banned but it only has caused an upsurge of defiance. This government must be politically extremely naïve. They ban hunting as a sop to their badly tarnished socialist roots but in doing so have united a mass of forces against them. Not only the wealthy who have traditionally hunted - and although sometimes I am not keen on some of their more arrogant members I respect the right of traditions to be maintained. Along with them is a class of rural people who see their way of life being eroded by modern urban society and interpret this as a direct attack. This is not just the traditional farm workers who have always followed the pack but a much larger swell of people who just don't see the need for the government to interfere - especially, dare it be whispered, when they appear to be bend over backwards to positively protect and encourage the traditions and ways of life to those who have only come to this old country in the past 50 years or so. Hunting has been a rural activity at least since the days of mediaeval kings.

There used to be a hunt kennels in the woods a little to the south of East Pennard you can still see foundations in red brickwork which are alleged to be a part of them. Silas would have certainly seen the hunt out and about whilst doing his rounds and is almost certain to have been swept into the excitement of the followers, spotting foxes as they slink across in front of him ahead of the chase.

I hear a cock crow. A rather flat and badly out of tune cockerel. I now see a couple of pens in a garden where someone must keep a few ornamental poultry as a hobby. In Silas's day many cottagers would have kept some bantams to provide eggs and every farmyard would have had poultry wandering around scratching here and there. Even when I started calling on farms 25 years ago this was not the unusual sight it is today now the government have placed all sorts of inspection regulations on the selling of even a few eggs from the farm gate.

As we approach the village the parkland style plantings increase with a selection of mature evergreens, tall cedars and pines and shorter squatter evergreen oaks. On my left now the old walled garden of Pennard House. This is where the vegetables and flowers for the house would originally have been grown. Now it is the home of Pennard Plants, a nursery growing a fine selection of herbaceous plants still using the wall delineated area of the former garden.

As the road slopes down the outbuildings of Pennard House come into view fronted by a massive ancient beech tree. Pennard House is right in the centre of the small village but protected within its own private park surrounded by a stonewall or iron railings. Beside the wall is the luxury of a pavement of stone flags raised slightly above the level of the road. In Silas's time this must have been a boon. The roads then would have been surfaced with crushed stone pounded flat. However in the winter the wheels of carts and hooves of horses would have soon rucked it up and the surface become pitted and muddy.

Down on through the village street. Behind a wall is the large Victorian Rectory which would have been newly built when Silas first started his round. Past the attractive little church room which now acts as a very small village hall. I once gave a demonstration of hanging basket making here, making an especially fragrant one for an elderly blind woman. It was good to feel a good community spirit in this small locality. The entire population is smaller than an urban road yet you got the feeling there was as much going on as there would be in a small town.

The road swings down and there in an almost dell like setting sits the attractive, if slightly dilapidated, Old Post Office - as a hand drawn notice on the front door states. This would have been an important point on Silas's round. I hope he got a cup of tea here - I know I certainly could do with one. He would also have off loaded a fair amount of post. I had been concerned as to how on earth he could have covered the whole of the Pennard parish which stretches over a massive area in both directions. Away to the northwest is Pennard Hill to the southwest Hembridge, Withial and Parbrook - the latter almost as big a village. Even further south the outlying farms at Stone and the Inn on the Fosseway. However on the 1881 census I spot a 16-year-old boy who is employed as a post boy. I suspect he may well have taken the mails to some of the more outlying areas. Silas would have come to this Sub Post Office twice a day - perhaps he ate his lunch here and had a sit down to rest his feet.

To Silas his boots must have been extremely important. I know I am wearing a rather heavy pair of old work boots that are a bit past their prime. I can already feel my feet. Silas must have been a bit like my old grandfather who took great care of his boots. He had a working pair and a going-out pair. The former he was always rubbing dubbin into and the latter forever polishing. To Silas, on his seventeen-mile walk every day, boots must have been crucial. They would have needed to be all leather and he must have done his most to keep them protected. Breaking in a new pair must have been something to dread so he would have kept his boots repaired as long as possible.

I climb up a steep slope and in the farmyard to my left see a small farm shop which I had not previously known existed. I assume it sells home-made cheese

No. 5.—EAST PENNARD, SOMERSET

The luxury of a raised pavement in Pennard. (postcard Adrian Pearse)

- there are still a lot of cheese makers in this locality though most now operate on a slightly larger scale than the description 'farmhouse' conjures up. In Silas's time nearly all the farms would have made cheese and the cheese factors would have come around to buy it from them to put in the storehouses in Stoney Stratton or Shepton Mallet before sending on to the city markets. It being Christmas Eve this farm shop appears to be doing a good trade - well two middle-aged female customers pull up as I walk past - both co-incidentally driving Volvos.

On my right is the little former village school. If it had been playtime Silas may well have exchanged greetings with the lively young children. However more often he would have heard then chanting their tables in class or the disciplined voice of the schoolmistress. This school has now been converted to residential use.

Two horses with female riders pass me in the lane; a four-wheel drive vehicle also showing politeness gently eases past. Silas of course would have seen many horses either being ridden or pulling carts, gigs, wagons or carriages. Most would have been going about business or at least on a journey to or from somewhere. However it is likely that there would have been people out from Pennard House riding for pleasure as these horses are being ridden now - however if there had been ladies aboard it is almost certain that they would have been riding side-saddle.

Here a track leads off to the right to Hembridge Farm. Silas may have gone down here and across to the other cottages in the hamlet of Hembridge and to Parbrook beyond but I suspect this south west quarter of the parish was the domain of the post boy.

There is a very noisy flock of starlings almost covering a small tree ahead. The views now open out to the south and even though it is a somewhat grey morning you can still see a long distance. Ham Hill and the hills before Yeovil in south Somerset are presumably the next major ridge however beyond that you can clearly see the distinctive shapes of Lewsdon and Pilsdon Pen in Dorset around 30 miles ahead, and less than ten miles from the sea at Bridport and Lyme Regis.

A huge buzzard is sat in a low tree but when I am a few yards away he appears to fall into flight with a couple of lazy flaps of his broad wings, glides low over a hedge and gaining height languidly flies away through another cider orchard. This one is properly riddled with mistletoe. It amazes me that with such a profusion around us we seem to need to import the majority of what is for sale in the shops from France.

The lane emerges on to a slightly broader lane that winds its way along the southern foot of the Pennard ridge from Glastonbury and the orchards of West Bradley. I turn left into Wraxall. There are a few houses and bungalows on either side of the road here but I am not sure that any of these would have been here in Silas's time. The older part of Wraxall is across the other side of the A37 and ahead of me I can see the Queens Arms but I have a diversion which I am sure Silas would have taken first.

A lane to the right leads down to Huxham Green. I pass Ash Farm which reminds me that there were a lot more smaller farms in the scattered outlying parts of East Pennard compared to the two big farms of Pylle. Here we are entering the low lands where farmers would have had a constant struggle with heavy soils and drainage in what was once the headlands of the Somerset moors across the low vale to Lydford about five miles ahead.

Huxham Green is a scattered collection of farms around a green central area. Over 100 years ago George Richards was a well respected-farmer here, breeding his dairy short horns and well known as a horse breeder. A descendant, Peter Richards, is still at Little Huxham Farm and still well known in horse circles. Taking a set of jumps from one horse event to another and trading in hay and feed. His blue lorry a familiar sight in the locality.

The centre of Huxham Green looks a little bit of a mess at the moment. Building work is being carried out to convert the Victorian farm buildings of Huxham Farm into yet more desirable residences. Although we may regret the passing of many farms and the characterless design of the square grey farm shed buildings today we must also be glad that these attractive redundant buildings have found a new lease of life and are being preserved - as long as the conversions are being done sympathetically.

I disturb a group of half a dozen large rabbits who have been grazing on a patch of grass. I see their white tails rising and falling as they rapidly disperse to safer hiding places. I wonder if Silas every made use of his bag to take some illicitly-gained rabbits back to a ready market in Shepton Mallet. Even if he didn't trap them himself I am sure his close involvement with the rural community would have bought at least a few rabbits his way.

Ahead is a narrow lane which I know leads out into the wilds. In the past I have visited a little cottage a good half mile further along where an elderly lady lived in the middle of nowhere. I couldn't believe that I could have got into such a deserted rural wilderness but still be less than a mile from the main Fosseway. In days gone past there were a couple more cottages down there when it was known as Hucky Mead

There is a lane that goes back directly to the Fosse and Silas may have gone that way to Stone and the Travellers Rest Inn but I can already hear the roar of traffic and knowing that section is very fast, despite a fictitious 40 mph limit, with virtually no verge I admit that safety is the better part of valour and return up the lane I have come down. Part of the reason for the narrowness of the Fosse Way here is that squatters' cottages were obviously built at some time within the traditional width of the road. You can easily identify them. They have virtually no land in front or to the rear but long thin gardens running alongside the Fosse.

Have just said "good morning" to John Fry - the Chief Executive of Yeovil Town Football club who was starting his car. I did know he lived around here but it still gave me a bit of a surprise. Now crossing the busy road to the Queen's Arms and the rest of the hamlet of Wraxall, a collection of grey stone farms and cottages. This is actually the western part of the parish of Ditcheat but as it is clearly mentioned on reports of Silas's round I am sure he delivered here. Although there was no Sub Post Office I suspect he must have had an arrangement either at the pub or at one of the cottages for somewhere to pick up some letters and maybe have a cup of tea.

I use my mobile phone to ring my son in Shepton Mallet and as pre-arranged ask

The Queen's Arms in Wraxall. The Fosseway was certainly quieter in Silas's day (postcard Adrian Pearse)

him to come and pick me up. It will take him little more than ten minutes to get here. As I sit on the wall of the Queen's Arms car park I think back over the morning. I have been walking for very nearly three hours at quite a good pace but it must be remembered that I have only done a couple of the probable side diversionary routes Silas would have had to cover. I haven't walked down a single driveway or up any garden paths. I haven't delivered a single letter. I haven't collected a single letter. Beyond a couple of "hellos" I haven't stopped for a single conversation. My legs are beginning to feel quite tired. Silas would now be only half done. He probably would set off from Wraxall up the steep hill of the Fosseway and on a roundabout route, calling at both East Pennard and Pylle Sub Post Offices, and work his way back to Shepton. He certainly did a good day's work and he would have covered this route over 330 times a year - getting only every second Sunday off. To have done this for nearly 40 years is dedication indeed - yet the glowing tributes both at his retirement and death suggest that in carrying out his work he had a rich and fulfilling life.

Silas - getting to know his customers

Having identified a probable route for his round it is now time to have a look at his customers - the people who lived on his round to whom he would have been delivering letters. Doing the same round for forty years, in those days when hours were longer, Silas would have got to know the families well. He would have seen children born, grow up, get married and have children of their own. In the space of forty years it is quite probable that their children in turn would be growing up and maybe ready to breed the next generation.

A remarkable description of Silas on his round has survived in the testament given by local farmer Joseph Board to Silas when presenting a purse of gold from the local people at the time of his retirement in 1908. A cutting from the Shepton Mallet Journal of 11 October reads:

'....he had known the latter (Silas) 34 or 35 years. His exceedingly courteous and pleasant manner - the same genial smile was always on his face - his half-military salute and sprightly step gave one the impression that his pay was excellent, and his duties light (laughter and applause). It was a pleasure to be able to bear witness to his indomitable courage and perseverance in all winds and weathers. The speaker had seen him trudging along knee-deep in snow, or when the roads had been a glare of ice, but never heard a murmur escape his lips....'

For the purposes of this exercise we will take one of the census years - 1881 and attempt to match the entries to Silas's round. Today most people tend to consider censuses only in their value to the family historian as a source of information about individuals and families. In fact with a bit more work they enable you to draw a picture of a complete society and tell you much of their lives and work.

One notable feature is that the census figures confirm the gentle decline of the rural population over this period. On April 22 1881 the Shepton Mallet Journal gives the official figures from that year's census and compares them to 1871. I have looked at the 1901 census and added the figures myself and by combining the two have arrived at the following.

	1871	1881	1901
Pylle	213	267	203
East Pennard	622	608	500

These should not be taken as gospel as there appear to be some inconsistencies in the area covered in the enumeration districts, for instance part of East Pennard seems to have been handed to West Bradley between 1871 and 1881 - however there is a reasonably clear trend.

Another way of painting an overall picture of a community is looking at what work the inhabitants were doing. For Pylle there were 107 people who had jobs identified. 64 (60%) of these were working in agriculture including 5 farmers, 35 agricultural labourers, 8 agricultural carters, 9 dairy workers, 2 shepherds, 3 bailiffs and a few other miscellaneous agricultural occupations. 20 (19% of the working population were in domestic service: 9 domestic servants, 3 gardeners, 3 cooks, 2 grooms etc. 23 (21%) were involved in a variety of other occupations ranging from railway workers though to Rector. We will discover more of these when we examine the census in more detail.

East Pennard presents a slightly different picture. Here out of a working population of 233 only 116 (50%) fractionally under half were employed in agriculture although this included 19 farmers a significantly higher proportion than in Pylle suggesting straight away that this was an area of more small farms. There were 86 agricultural labourers but only 10 people specifically identified as dairy workers and only 1 farm bailiff. Here 60, or 26% of the working population, were in domestic service though it would appear that with 9 servants living in and another 9 living out, Pennard House with 18 was more than responsible by itself for the increased percentage. The 57 (24%)'others' is a similar proportion to Pylle but included a wider range of occupations which will again be looked at in more detail.

One immediately noticeable feature is that by and large married women did not work. There were exceptions, particularly with dairy workers where it was more the norm to be a husband and wife - or indeed a family affair. However most other working women were single - either in domestic service or working alone as a laundress or a dressmaker.

Another very noticeable feature is the very high proportion of the population who were born locally. Most families came from either Pylle or East Pennard - though not necessarily the one in which they currently lived. This was followed by people from other adjoining rural parishes such as West Pennard, Lottisham, Lydford, Doulting or Pilton. It would be wrong to paint a picture of a static population however. With agricultural workers there were plenty of instances of people coming from other parts of Somerset or Wiltshire. When it came to other crafts, and particularly professional residents (Rectors, school teachers etc) it was more normal for people to come from outside the locality entirely.

This picture of a largely farming and rural population is as would be expected.

According to the books on rural history, (examples mentioned in the book list at the end,) it is widely agreed that the period from the early 1870s up until 1900, and then with slightly less intensity up to the commencement of the Great War in 1914, is known as the 'Great Agricultural Depression.' A previously commonly accepted idea that people had been forced off the land by the enclosure movement of the 'agricultural revolution' from the period from 1760 to 1860 has largely been proved false. The statistics show that although the populations of towns and cities were rising fast the number of people employed in agriculture also kept on rising to increase agricultural output to feed those in towns.

The most common theory now is that from the early 1870s a series of weather affected harvests combined with the importation of large quantities of grain from the newly opened-up American mid-west and other food imports from Ireland, Holland, Denmark and France led to a severe depression for British farming leading to a sharp decline in the number of people employed in agriculture. The national figures show that as a proportion of national produce agriculture was continuing to decline in significance. This decline was most severe in the traditional grain growing areas of the east and southeast. The pastoral areas of the West Country escaped the worst through focusing on producing milk and dairy products for the growing city markets where an increase in real wages resulted in an improved demand for better foods. However many social historians still go to great lengths to paint a dark picture of rural poverty and deprivation. The suggestion is that the decline of the farm population would have been just as bad in these areas as pastoral farming used less labour than grain farming. Therefore, due to lack of jobs, poverty was great and labourers were forced off the land to either emigrate or find work in the cities; those left on the land supposedly being the poorest specimens who lacked ambition.

It would be expected that an occupation analysis of the 1901 census for East Pennard and Pylle would support this theory - especially as we already know that the population had reduced by about a fifth. What we actually find is somewhat surprising.

East Pennard and Pylle	1881	%	1901	%
Total Population	875		705	
Working population	340	39%	289	41%
Of which				
Farming	180	53%	171	59%
Domestic Service	80	24%	54	19%
Other	80	24%	64	22%

Against expectations the percentage of the population working in farming has actually risen and despite a decline of nearly 20% in the total population there has only been a decline of about 5% in the number of people employed in agriculture. This is hardly indicative of large numbers of people being driven off the land.

The sharpest decline in working population seems to be amongst those in domestic service. This could well be suggestive that things were not as prosperous as previously. There certainly do appear to be fewer servants employed on the larger farms. The decline in people in 'other' jobs seems to be more proportional to the decline in the population as a whole. However closer analyses shows that much of this reduction seems to come in jobs for women. There were no laundresses, of whom there were six in 1881, only two dressmakers, against six. Also gone were 2 glovers and one seamstress. All the 'village crafts', carpenters, shoemakers, blacksmiths, butchers and bakers seem to have survived intact. There is very little evidence for any significant breakdown in the rural economy.

It would be wrong to come to any great conclusions for economic trends elsewhere from this very limited survey of two small adjacent rural parishes. If we did the analysis ten years either side perhaps we would come to different figures. However what we can suggest is that for the time that Silas was delivering the letters the rural communities, which he daily walked through, remained fundamentally the same.

Pylle

We now try to follow Silas's round through the 1881 census. We start our tour at what is now called Hedge Lane. Although Hedge Farm always appears to have been at the end of the lane this does not seem to have always been the name of the lane. On the 1880s Ordnance Survey map it is marked as Bryants Lane and this is how the census refers to it, however it also mentions Silver Street which seems be the cottages on the main Fosse Road at that end of Bryants Lane to the north of Street-on-the-Fosse.

Amongst these cottages are those known as Duke Cottages which on later censuses were referred to as 'The Old Duke' and are now presumably Duke Farm. In 1881 one was inhabited by Paul March - as we will see very much the local name at that time. The latest phone book still shows a number of March's living in Pylle and East Pennard. Paul March was a 34 year old 'engine tenter'. Also referred to a 'tender', this was someone who looked after and agricultural traction engine which travelled from farm to farm. This would most probably have been a threshing machine which was in common use to thresh gain from the mid nineteenth century until the second word war when combine harvesters (combining cutting, threshing and straw baling) made them redundant. The other possibility is that is he could have worked a steam ploughing outfit. Paul had a 13-year old son at home who was at work as an agricultural labourer.

Next door in Duke cottages was George Higgins, another local name, who was a 67-year old pauper. Living with him was his 15 year old grandson who once again was an agricultural labourer. At the other Duke cottage lived William

Reproduced from 1907 Ordnance Survey map with kind permision of the Ordnance Survey

Ridout a 56 year old thatcher. He is the first person mentioned who was not born locally coming from West Stour in Wiltshire. It would be wrong to assume that the main role of a thatcher was to thatch roofs. At that time most thatching would have been on ricks of corn or hay which needed to be protected from the elements until it was time to thresh them. This was usually spread through the winter months and the threshing machine would come in to a farm to thresh a rick at a time as the grain was needed - mainly to feed to animals.

The next three cottage that Silas would have come to were collectively known as Hedge Cottages. In one lived James Biggins a 50 year old carter / agricultural labourer. All farm produce at that time would have had to be carted, if only to the railway station down the road, and farm carts were a common sight in the countryside. As James was also identified as an agricultural labourer it is likely that he was employed by the local farm and put to other uses when there was no carting to do. His 20 year old son Thomas was living at home and working as an under carter / agricultural labourer.

Another of Hedge Cottages was occupied by Edward Crunton a 53 year old farm bailiff, today this role would most likely be called a manager, usually the farmers right hand man where a farmer took an active interest in the farm, as opposed to an 'agent' who would be more likely to run the farm for an absentee farmer / landowner.

The occupant of the third Hedge cottage is bit of a puzzle. He is 44 year old John Higgins who although having a local name was born in London. He is described as a 'Landowner'. This is an unusual appellation. Local historian Adrian Pearce has revealed that he was an interesting local character. A member of the Stockwood Farm Higgins family, he was a well educated man who produced Shakespearean plays at Castle Cary amongst other literary pursuits. His 69 year old mother lives with him and is an 'annuitant' - someone who is in receipt of a pension, she also was born in London. Living in Hedge Cottages with no servants it seems very unlikely that he was a wealthy person. Perhaps his father was a local person who had gone to London and got some property and his son was now living of the modest rental income?

Silas would pass the Wesleyan Chapel. Next to this lived James Dredge a 65-year old farmer and dairyman whose daughter Elizabeth, 26, was working as a dairywoman. No acreage is shown in this census but checking back to 1871 he was then shown as farming 20 acres with a wife and one daughter.

An interesting entry here is that 1881 James's 37 year old son, John Dredge, was visiting at the time of the census. He is described as a cab driver - London. It will be noticed as we continue this survey that there appear to be less people in the 25 - 35 age group. The conventional theory is that the agricultural depression drove people from the land and they had to go to the cities to find work. It is probably a bit more complex than this. Here we are still in the early years of the agricultural depression but John would seem to be one of many who are already 'missing' but are still in contact with their family. As he was not present in the 1871 census he is quite likely to have already moved to London before the agricultural depression set in. There are a number of instances where it is possible to see families that have been away and have later come back. It is possible that there was as much of a 'pull' element for young people looking for wider opportunities and experience in an expanding economy as there was the 'push' factor of lack of jobs and poverty. The example of Paul March above as an engine tenter suggests there were still opportunities for people looking to stay locally.

It is also interesting to see that John Dredge was working in London as a cab driver. G E Mingay in 'Rural Life in Victorian England' mentions that this role, working with horses, was one that was popular and more suited to rural people moving into cities than it was to the city dwellers.

Next door was Robert Higgins 62 an Army pensioner and agricultural labourer living with his son Job, 17 an agricultural labourer. He may well have had more children previously but they would have left home. The majority of children leaving home would at this time have been marrying locally and starting their own families - the ease with which local names can be spotted is testament to this. Given his age it is quite probable that Robert was a veteran of the Crimean War.

81-year-old Elizabeth Foote is the head of the next household and is described as infirm. However living with her are two grand-daughters - Ann Osbourne 20 and Elizabeth Foote 16 - both are described as domestic servants.

Next door again and seemingly on the corner of Hedge Lane is Thomas Baby a 60-year old farm bailiff who had been born in Scotland but had married a local girl and settled in the area. In 1871 he was listed as an agricultural labourer. By 1901 he was living at Silver Head - which may well be the same cottage - and aged 80, still with his 79 year old wife Ann. It would be nice to think of Silas stopping morning and afternoon as he passed to have a quick chat about the local scene with Thomas; Thomas's Scottish burr contrasting to the broad west country accent of Silas.

Going up 'Bryants' Lane we come to Hedge Farm which presumably had only relatively recently been built by the Portman estate. Here we find William Cary 49 described as 'farmer and cheese merchant.' The cheese merchant is an important aspect of local agriculture. William Cary was one of an important local farming family and there are still many Carys farming in mid Somerset though direct connections are often hard to trace. They were also amongst the prominent cheese factors who were responsible for spreading the hygiene and production controls which first produced a consistent Cheddar cheese that we would recognize today. Another local cheese factor - Hills at nearby Stoney Stratton - produced an instruction leaflet for their farmer suppliers, also local farmer's daughter Edith Cannon at Milton Clevedon near Evercreech set up some early cheese making schools which eventually led to the establishment of Cannington Agricultural College.

The Carys had a big factors cheese store in Shepton Mallet which operated as such into the middle of the last century. They bought up cheese from local farms to supply into the city markets. As we carry on this tour we should bear in mind that many of the local farmers would also have been cheese makers using milk they produced on their own farms, and that these farms would have been at the forefront of their industry. The Mid Somerset Show in Shepton Mallet and the Frome Cheese Show were considered the leading two cheese shows outside London.

The census records that William Cary farmed 480 acres, which would still be considered as a large farm for this area today. He was a tenant of the Portman Estate which owned most of the parish. He employed 12 men and 4 boys from the surrounding cottages. He lived with his wife and two daughters who were 18 and 16. Being a man of some substance he also has two live-in servants, Eliza York 25, described as a cook / domestic servant and Emily Marshman 18, housemaid.

In a nearby cottage on the farm lived James Howell the shepherd. Like many of the farm workers with more specific skills he was not a local being born near the Wiltshire, Somerset and Dorset borders at Stourton. His 22 year old daughter who was a domestic servant had been born in Gillingham. Boarding with them was 23 year old groom / gardener Walter Drew who, one would assume, worked for the farm.

Across the fields at the end of the lane at what is now known as Old Hedge Farm, then known as Hedge Dairy, where 33-year old Charles Griffin and his wife Jane were dairyman and dairywoman. They would probably have run the dairy for Mr Cary, but with a young family, the nursegirl and servant living there may have been in their own employ. There was also John Marsh a 17 year old cowman shown as part of the household. Although we don't know of the exact relationship in this instance it is possible that Charles Griffin would have had a fair amount of autonomy from the farm - running the dairy as his own business under contract to the farmer. Such arrangements were fairly frequent in the late 19th century.

From here Silas would probably have cut across the fields to Street-on-the-Fosse which represents the main centre of population of the small parish of Pylle. He would have come first to the railway station where Thomas Alexander aged 26 was the head of household and station master. In this census three people were identified as working for the railway. Living just along the road was 19 year old Walter Penny described as a 'railway signalman.' He lived at home with his father 48 year old Thomas Penny described as a 'portable engine driver.' Presumably this referred to a traction engine which may have been used for heavy haulage or agricultural work. The other railway worker was the lodger at the household of Eliza March a 69 year old pauper. He was 22 year old George Norman from Ashwick who was identified as a 'railway clerk'

Next to the station is the Portman Hotel where William Moody aged 61 is described as 'auctioneer, farmer and inn keeper.' Such joint occupations were quite common - especially amongst publicans. The Moodys were a local farming family and William's business as an auctioneer was quite substantial. Local directories show him as well as having an 'office' in Pylle also having an 'office' at the Hare and Hounds in Shepton Mallet. Newspaper advertisements show him running livestock auctions in Castle Cary, Evercreech Junction as well as repository sales out of the Portman Hotel. By the time of the 1891 census he had

A view of the cottages at Street-on-the-fosse. (postcard Joe King)

died but his wife Elizabeth Moody a 64 year old widow was then listed as Hotel Proprietor whilst son John (31) was an 'auctioneer / valuer / estate agent.'

Near to the Portman Hotel is the blacksmiths - so speculation about the siting of the current petrol garage is probably correct. Walter Garland aged 29 was the blacksmith - showing again that there were still rural opportunities for younger people. The Garlands are a noted family of farmers and blacksmiths. O V Garland and Son, originally a blacksmith in the nearby village of North Wootton still operate, selling dairy milking equipment. The household next door to the blacksmiths is that of Charles Coates who was a coachman. Living here it is possible that his business was tied to the railway station rather than a large house.

Most of the cottages in Street-on-the-Fosse where inhabited by agricultural labourers and their families. No fewer than 16 heads of household were either 'ag labs' or 'ag lab / carter.' Seven of the heads of households in this area of the parish had the surname March, whilst another five bore the name Biggins and three Higgins. Apart from agricultural labourers we find a few other occupations. Sarah Biggins (69) is described as a shop keeper, John Fry (45) is a carpenter. Next is the school, already in the purpose built building now used as the village hall, William Biggins who is listed as a butcher dealer whilst his wife Susan (43) was the schoolmistress.

Given the small size of many of the cottages there is an incredible number of lodgers. Some were relatives, others were workers, probably working locally for a short time. These included an agricultural drainer (foreman journeyman) who would have been contracted by farmers to install drainage systems to fields, two timber hauliers, a lime burner, and a shepherd.

There does not appear to have been a Post Office of any sort in Pylle at this time. However by 1891 the Susan Biggins who is listed as the school teacher in 1881 is now listed as the Postmistress. Her husband William Biggins is still listed as a butcher, however they would appear to be living next door to the station master at that time. By 1901 the Post Office is once more associated with the school and on the early Ordnance survey maps appears to be actually in the school building just around the corner in Pylle Lane. Robert Avery 59 from Portsmouth is listed as certified school master, his wife Sarah (66) is Sub-Post Mistress whilst their daughter Ellen (30) is given as a teacher in school. Silas would have had to call here twice a day to collect the mail.

From Street on the Fosse Silas probably had to do a couple of diversions. He

The Manor House, Pylle. (postcard Richard Raynsford)

may have had to take the road east towards Evercreech to Lower Easton Farm which was actually in East Pennard where the parish boundary looped out round to surround Pylle on nearly three sides. Lower Easton Farm was farmed by 45 year old James Dredge who looked after171 acres employing 5 men and 1 boy. Still a significant farm for the period but small compared to the two huge estate farms of Pylle. Beyond this was the railway cottage at Elbow Corner where John Griffin 35 is described as a 'railway labourer' - one assumes he was a level crossing keeper.

Silas would also have had to go carry on up the Fosse which rose quite steeply here. He would have had to go to Writh Farm where at this time lived 45 year old John Treasure a dairyman and in Writh cottage James March an agricultural labourer. It is quite probable that at this time Writh was a dairy operating under the Manor Farm at Pylle. In 1891 Cornelius Barber (41) described as a 'dairy manager' lived there with his wife and two daughters working in the dairy. Barber is still a very significant name for dairy farming and cheese making in the adjoining parish of Ditcheat.

Silas would have also delivered at the eight cottages on Pye Hill. These would seem to have been mainly lived in by agricultural labourers and quite small - only one had more than two people in them. They also included a cordwainer and James Hoare who at 66 is listed as a road contractor. Road mending seems to have been a quite regular form of employment for elderly men - presumably being paid enough money to break rocks to repair roads and keep them above the poverty line and out of the workhouse. Silas may also have had to go to Easton Hill Farm on the top of the hill before returning to Street on the Fosse and taking the lane to Pylle itself.

In 1881 Silas would have found the church, the Rectory, the Manor House and only about three other cottages. The Manor House was at this time a working farm - the buildings, as they still are, extremely adjacent for what appears a very grand house. The farmer - a tenant for the Portman estate, was 37-year old Edmund Cary who farmed an absolutely massive 880 acres with twenty-four men and 4 boys. This was a very substantial farming operation for the area and he was by a long way the leading local employer. His household included wife and family and also a cook as well as a domestic servant indicating that he was a person of some substance. Of the local cottages James March (49) carter/ ag lab and John Cabbell (63) farm bailiff almost certainly worked for him. John Cabbell's 20 year old daughter Mary was the infant school teacher.

East Pennard historian Adrian Pearse has found that the Carys had previously been tenants of the 100 acre Pennard Hill Farm East Pennard (then called Proctors Farm) so they were a family who had certainly done well for themselves.

THE RECTORY, PYLLE.

The rectory at Pylle - definately a gentlemans residence. (postcard Joe King)

The farm is farmed by a Cary today but he is not a direct descendant of this line of the family.

The other significant house Silas would have to have delivered to is The Rectory, home of Henry F B Portman (41) rector of Pylle. He was a younger son of the Portman Family. In 1871 he was already here but then with a wife, son and daughter who are not present in 1881. It would need further investigation to find out what had happened to them. In 1901 there is another a strange circumstance with Charles McConnel 45 the clergyman at The Rectory whilst his wife Beatrice McConnel (34) 'clergyman's wife' lives with three children and servants at Pylle Hill Cottage. Henry Portman in 1881 has the appearance of being gentry, Joe King's photograph of the gracious rectory shows the standard of accommodation. Living with him in 1881 was his 35 year old sister, Mary Hubbard (38) cook and Thyrza Gollege (21) parlour maid, whilst at Rectory Lodge lived Henry March (66) gardener, his wife Sara (66) lodge keeper, and a boarder George Mabey a groom.

From Pylle Silas would have had to turn north down the Pilton lane for about half a mile to the lime works. Here in 1881 the 'foreman of the lime burning works' was a James Faull (22) from Cornwall with a his boarder William Lewis (19) from Dorset. The reason for quite such young men being so far from their place of birth would appear to be a bit of an oddity. Lime burning was quite a common occupation in this locality. Although there is the possibility that Silas may have had to cross the fields to reach the farm / dairy at Cockmill it more likely that he now returned to Pylle and climbed the steep gully to Little Pennard.

East Pennard

Presumably because of the intertwined nature of the parish boundaries some of Little Pennard appears on the Pylle Census and some on East Pennard. In the Pylle portion was the household of Richard Osbourne 41, who is listed as a 'baker and corndealer.' He had working for him three sons between the age of 19 and 16. Given the remoteness of the location from many other cottages it is more than likely that they had bakers rounds delivering around the local villages and probably into Shepton Mallet.

The East Pennard section of Little Pennard contained another four households - which may well be more than today. One was a 70-year old or widow Alice Goodland who is listed as a pauper. Pauperism was a serious problem for the elderly in the days before the state old age pension was introduced in 1908. Some would have sadly ended in the workhouse but in the village there do appear to have been ways to keep them in their old cottages. In fact although this is the time of the so-called 'Great Agricultural Depression' there is not a huge amount of evidence of rural pauperism in the census. Some of the few instances mentioned seem to be related to mental or physical infirmity - but again they seem to be found places to live within their local community.

Little Pennard also contained a farmer, Stephen Mullins who was farming a significant 200 acres and employed two dairywomen who lived in. The final

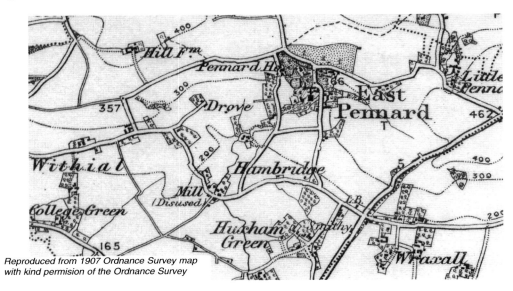

*Reproduced from 1907 Ordnance Survey map
with kind permision of the Ordnance Survey*

Country house living - Pennard House. (postcard Adrian Pearse)

household was that of Thomas Harte a 40-year old blacksmith and his wife Elizabeth who had at home 8 children between the ages of 12 and 1 year old. Little Pennard for a small hamlet would seem to have been a remarkably active and productive place.

From here Silas would probably have walked down the lane towards the small village area of East Pennard itself. This was dominated by Pennard House the long time home of the Napier family. The list of residents at the 1881 census paints a picture of country house life of a time long past.

Edward B Napier	Head	64	Magistrate	Born	East Pennard
Emily	Wife	54			Chelsea
Gerard	Son	23	Magistrate		London
Edward	Son	19	Undergraduate Oxford		London
Effie	Dau	12	Scholar		East Pennard
Gerard	Brother	62	Vice Admiral RN		East Pennard
Ellen	Bro wife	49			Chelsea
Ella	Niece	16			Southsea
Johanna Hintish	Governess	28	Governess		Germany
Walter Trevelyan	Visitor	41	Clergyman Church of England		Sussex
George Batten	Serv	26	Footman		West Lydford
Margaret Mathias	Serv	32	Cook Housekeeper		Cardigan
Sarah Robin	Serv	36	Ladies Maid		Street

Sophia Alford	Serv	55	Housemaid	Somerset ?
Mary Liscombe	Serv	22	Laundry Maid	Devon
Maude Price	Serv	27	Kitchen Maid	Birmingham
Mary Matthews	Serv	16	Housemaid	Devon
Verletta Spenser	Serv	19	School room maid	Cornwall

In addition to this there were many members of staff such as gardeners and grooms living in the surrounding houses. I suspect Silas might have enjoyed delivering to the big house. Did he go to the back door or up to the front to pass a few comments with the footman?

The houses in what is referred to in the census as 'Pennard Street' include an interesting selection of inhabitants. John Yeoman 58, is an agricultural labourer and sexton of the Church, Stephen Rossiter 30, is an agricultural labourer whilst his wife, Henrietta is a dressmaker. Neighbour Stephen Underwood 57 is another agricultural labourer whose wife is employed, Sarah was a laundress. Charles Yeoman 36 was a gardener, William Dyer 50 a coachman and one of his sons Charles 16 a stable boy whilst another Harry (twins?) is a letter carrier. George Hucker, 48 is the local policeman - I suspect he covered quite a wide area. John Hopkins 41, is a carter whilst Robert Phelps 30 was another agricultural labourer. Then at the Post Office is William Radnage 58 and his wife Hannah 57. William is described as a carpenter and Post Master.

The Rectory at East Pennard. (postcard Adrian Pearse)

Silas would have made his way to East Pennard Sub Post Office on his way through in the morning and back during the afternoon. I conjecture that he is likely to have left post here which Harry Dyer the 16 year old letter carrier would have then taken around the western parts of the Parish of East Pennard - which includes Pennard Hill, Withial, Drove, Bull Plot, Forge Well, Hembridge and Blind Stile. This was an area largely consisting of scattered farms and agricultural cottages. The discovery of a letter carrier rather confirmed my concern that there was no way Silas could cover the whole parish. The subsequent reports in the Shepton Mallet Journal refer to him walking 17 miles a day, and refer to this as being further than he was officially credited. Having measured the route by car and allowing for diversions the route described best matches that distance and is the most probable.

Adrian Pearse lives in Hill Farm Pennard where his family has farmed for over 60 years - just outside the area I think Silas delivered to. However Adrian has pointed out that in the 1880s Joe Board farmed here. Joe was the farmer who gave the description of Silas quoted above and knew him well. However I do not think this is incompatible with this being outside the core area of Silas's round. Over the 40 years he was delivering to the parish it is more than likely that Silas would have got to know all of it well with periodic changes in the detail of his round and covering for sickness, holiday and other staff absences.

People with local knowledge may notice I have left out Parbrook which straddles the south westerly parish boundary and is split between East Pennard and West Bradley parishes. Allen Cotton a local historian from West Bradley is convinced that all of the post for Parbrook would have been delivered by the Glastonbury postal district and that at times Parbrook had its own sub Post Office with West Bradley.

Heading south through the village Silas would have passed the Rectory. In 1881 this was the home of quite an elderly incumbent, Adam Goldney, originally from Westminster. In 1881 he was 72 and his wife Mary 65. As his 29-year old daughter Ellen had been born in East Pennard he must have had a long tenure in the Parish. The size of the vicarage would suggest that he lived in some style and the fact that he had four live-in servants tends to confirm this.

Down the hill is Waterfall Cottage which was soon to become the Post Office. At that time is was lived in by John Webly 41, a butler. I would assume he was a servant at Pennard House who had the status to be allowed to live in a cottage rather than in the house.

Climbing the hill we come to Batch Farm where Henry Coles 40, farmed 93 acres with three men and his son. This is a very typical size of farm for the parish of

East Pennard where the farms where in general a lot smaller than in Pylle. There were 18 farmers altogether in East Pennard compared to just three in Pylle.

Up the hill in Yew Tree cottage lived labourer Matthew Day 51 and his wife. Lodging with them was Emma Fear 29 an assistant school teacher. The Board School house was next door but one where John Rossiter aged 36 lived. He was a gardener / domestic servant but his wife Mary Ann 37, was the Schoolmistress. Between these two houses was Yew Tree Villa where Edward Rapson 45, the Curate of East Pennard lived. Today the Parishes of Pylle, East Pennard and Ditcheat have for many years have one rector between them. In 1881 East Pennard alone could support not only a rector but a curate in sufficient style to have one live-in servant.

There were two more cottages along Pennard Lane. Both would appear to be people who would have worked at Pennard House, the major employer for the village. John Money 56, was a coachman and it is unlikely that anyone other than the Napiers would have employed coachmen. Next door was William Yeoman a 41 year old gardener.

From here Silas's route would have taken him downhill. It is possible that he struck off westwards' and delivered to the farms and hamlet of Hembridge. However as this would have been in the same direction as Parbrook which is almost certainly too far for him to have gone regularly it is more likely that he went to the hamlet of Huxham.

There were three farms around Huxham. The smallest was 67 acres and was farmed by Solomon Green 65 and his 24 year old son Charles. The other two farms were both 250 acres and farmed by prominent members of the farming community. George Richards 53 employed 6 men and 3 boys. John Day 35 is from another local farming family. Most interesting here is that his birth place is given as Orwell, Ohio. Without more research it is open to guesswork as to the reason for this. However given that he comes from a local farming family it is likely that his father had tried emigration and had later returned to England. This is a pattern that is evident quite frequently in a number of cases of local farmers emigrating to Canada or even Australia from this area, only to return when things didn't prove as golden as expected - or the lure of the family proved too strong.

Both of these farmers employed a live-in governess, to look after their children, and live-in servants. One of the contemporary observations of the great depression in agriculture in this period was that farmers tried to mimic the gentry. The suggestion is that they lived above themselves, didn't like to get their hands dirty and spent more time hunting and driving around in gigs than farming infering that the 'hardship' suffered was of their own making because of their more extravagant life style. It has already been suggested that farmers in this part of the country were less hard hit than in arable areas. However it is noticeable that although the number of farmers remained very similar in the 1901 census - they did appear to employ less domestic servants. However this may have been influenced by the fact that in a sample as small as this survey a number of farmers in their 30's and 40's and with young families in 1881 did not have the same need for servants 20 years later.

Also in Huxham we find our first stonemason, Isaac Snook, at the age of 77 he may have been getting past some of the heavy work but fortunately his son Adam 35, also a mason, lived with him. There are other masons along the road at Parbrook. Although there may have been a greater call for masons in towns they must also have been scattered throughout the countryside.

On occasion Silas may have had to go a nearly mile further south to Stone were there were two more farms and a number of agricultural labourers' households. In 1881 there was also a household headed by 65-year old widow Anne White who was specified as being on parish relief. This is another example of the poor not necessarily being sent straight to the workhouse.

On the Fosse Road itself we find 53 year old Edward Bulsure and his wife. He is described as a beer house keeper, undoubtedly at what is still the wayside inn The Travellers Rest. Lodging with him is William Taylor a blacksmith.

Back up the Fosse we come to the end of Silas's round in Wraxall. This was split between the two parishes of East Pennard on the west side of the road and Ditcheat on the east. Although it can never have been much more than a hamlet with no sign of being a village there is an interesting selection amongst its few households. There were two large farms Gollege's and Vincent's - both very prominent farmers in the Mid Somerset Agricultural Association. Tom Vincent and his son, also Tom, were to serve as officials for nearly 70 years between them. There was the Queens Arms and another beerhouse. There were two generations of blacksmith called Green, a family of shoemakers and two generations of a family of carpenters called Bennett. Quite a productive selection for so small a place.

Once here Silas would have been around halfway through his round. He is about seven miles from Shepton Mallet. It could be that he now went back up the Fosse over the top taking in the scattered farms at Easton on route though he would also have to return via the two Post Offices to collect any mail handed in during the day.

Silas the news carrier

From the reactions to him at the time of his retirement there is no doubt that Silas was a 'friend' to the people on his round. He knew them well and obviously had time whilst going about his duties to pass the time of day with them. One aspect of a postman's job, which we have lost in recent years of improved productivity, is that of the spreader of news. I remember speaking to a retired local farmer. In the days before the Second World War he said you didn't really need a newspaper because you saw the postman three times a day and at least once he would stop for a cup of tea. All the local news and gossip was passed rapidly around the community.

The people to whom Silas was delivering were also very likely to be much more interested in what was going on in their local community than we are today. The socialist historians may like to paint images of oppressed labour who had no time for thinking about anything other than being downtrodden by their greedy employers - but this appears to pay little relation to the reality. The evidence would tend to suggest that in Victorian society individuals led quite satisfying lives - aware of the past and the changes that were happening. Education was seen as important by many - both improvement for themselves and school for their children. Newspapers and books were becoming increasingly common. Worker founded reading rooms found their way even into the villages. Village clubs and self-help friendly societies were being formed.

Unlike today a person would have known a lot of the people in the surrounding villages - they had extended families and would have known their 1st and 2nd cousins - who they were married to and where they worked - unlike today when you may not be exactly sure what your sisters sons are up to. As late as the 1960s when I was a boy I knew old Joe the postman and John the milkman. They were people who came to the front door every day and if you passed them in the street they would say hello to you. We just do not on the whole have the same level of personal relationships today.

Admittedly the people on Silas's round wouldn't have the tremendous advantages we have today which allow us to keep contact with all that is considered to be so important in society through the constant availability of soaps, day time television and reality TV. They wouldn't have benefitted from the insight into the minds of cretinous 'celebs'. Nor would they have had the advantage of obesity packed prepared meals on the supermarket shelves. Even so it is just possible that rather than viewing people from this period as rural primitives, we should consider that they may in fact have had richer lives and minds than many people today.

Can we find out what sort of news they would have been talking about? What was the gossip that Silas would have been passing from house to house? Unfortunately most is lost in the vast ether of time. However it is possible to catch glimpses by looking through the pages of the Shepton Mallet Journal for 1881 and finding some of the key stories. The parish registers also reveal the births, deaths and marriages during the year. We can piece together something of the feel of the times.

Local papers at the time were somewhat different to those we are used to today. For a start they had a lot fewer pages - usually only four - but with an exceedingly small type there was a lot packed in. Advertisements probably played at least as important a role as they would today - though very few were set as 'display', linage adverts being more the norm. The news coverage and usually the editorial were surprisingly orientated to national matters and other regional news with local news probably making up less than 10% of the paper. The letters to the editor were most likely to be on a matter of religious or political philosophy. It would also be fair to say that the coverage of goings on in the villages was somewhat sporadic. Never the less what we do find are gems of social history.

7 January 1881. Silas would certainly have passed speculation as to who was likely to be the new tenant of Wraxall Villa. This week's paper carried an advertisement that the house and pasture was to be let at Lady Day 1881. It is described as a genteel residence together with suitable walled garden, two-stalled stable, coach house and 3 or 10 acres of good adjoining pasture land. Commanding aspect, well sheltered and watered situated at Wraxall, close to a good road and about two and a half miles from Pylle or Evercreech Junction on the Somerset and Dorset Line and 3 miles from Castle Cary on the Great Western Railway. Apply JC Gollege (the Owner) Wraxall House.

9 January. The first new baby of the year, for Silas to spread the news, was William Austin Moody a son for farmer William and his wife Elizabeth. William farmed at Withial in the east of East Pennard on 160 acres with 5 men and one boy. It was their third child.

14 January. The paper had news of foot and mouth outbreaks that would have been a major concern for Silas to discuss with the farmers. Foot and mouth rumbled on throughout the year but never seems to have made an appearance in the immediate locality. Even in those days the government were involved in helping stop the spread of the disease and magistrates were responsible for imposing restrictions on movements of livestock - in particular shutting livestock markets.

14 January. The Shepton Mallet Petty Sessions were as usual chaired by E B Napier Esq of Pennard House. Amongst the cases was one from neighbouring Pilton that would have caused amused discussion. Samuel Cox a timber haulier and dealer was charged with being drunk in charge of a horse and cart on Christmas Eve. The festive celebrations drink-drive problem is nothing new.

16 January. Silas would have been passing on the news of first son, William, for Charles and Mary Whithead an agricultural labourer who lived in the northeast of the parish near Cockmill.

21 January. For postmen, farmers and indeed anyone who lives in the British Isles the weather is a constant source of discussion. We are lucky enough to have one of the most variable climates in the world. As a postman Silas may have had rather too close a relationship with it but for many people in those days there was little getting away from it. As news it even quite regularly appeared in the Shepton Mallet Journal

'The Weather - We have something more than a ordinary occurrence to record under this heading this week for we have been visited by such a snow storm as has not been known in this area within the memory of living man.'

Silas must have been having a tough time. It followed on a fortnight of hard frosts that had given good skating on the local ponds. However, when the snow started it carried on all Monday, Monday night, all Tuesday and part of Wednesday and the whole time there was a high and variable wind which drifted the snow up to 10 feet in depth. As would be expected today the area came to a complete halt. Trains couldn't run, business and schools were shut and all roads were blocked. Cattle and sheep had to be dug out and all service pipes were frozen. It wasn't until the Thursday morning that the council managed to get gangs organized to try to clear the roads.

'The time for the poor has been most hard and even where thought least deserving a little charity now would not lose its reward. Fireless, pain-stricken, homeless and starving people have had more to endure than can easily be imagined or expressed. We commit such thoughts to our readers and feel sure that without an appeal for funds, many of these who are able to do so, will quietly and cheerfully send their nearer and poorer neighbours a meal for themselves and their families.'

21 January. With the Post Office only a couple of doors away from the offices of the Shepton Mallet Journal is it fanciful to imagine that it may have been Silas who bought the news of a terrible tragedy at Pylle into town? On the Tuesday

Pylle Station, scene of a terrible tragedy. (postcard Adrian Pearse)

morning orders were received for two railway workers to go from Pylle station to Evercreech Junction to help clear the snow. They set off along the line in blinding snow with only a yard visibility. They had only gone 100 yards when a train going in the opposite direction crashed into them both. One man - at first identified as William Sheppard but corrected the next week to William Humphries - died from terrible injuries three hours later. A second, Samuel March, although badly injured was able to give evidence at the enquiry a week later. - A verdict of 'Accidental death' was passed.

28 January. The weather was still the main topic 10 days after the start of the storm. A mild thaw had only just set in and people were still employed carting snow off roads, though many in rural districts were still blocked. The London mails did not arrive until the Friday and it was the weekend before a semblance of normal service resumed on the railways.

'A gradual thaw will be beneficial in diminishing the heaps of snow which surround us, and assisting to make roads passable, though to pedestrians the slush is a source of great unpleasantness. We only hope a flood will not occur.'

One suspects that the wiry Silas was invited in for many cups of tea when he managed to get through to deliver the mail to rural cottages anxious for news of how others were faring.

11 February. The weather was still the major topic of conversation. Where snow had drifted against the sides of buildings it had got in under the eaves and as it thawed had bought a lot of ceilings down. People living in the smaller cottages were said to have been 'sadly inconvenienced.'

Nor had the snow disappeared, at the beginning of the week it was said that some of the byways were still impassable. This was followed by more snow which changed to rain, wind and gales with 'trees, tiles and chimneystacks suffering from its violence. A postman's lot is sometimes not a happy one and even Silas must have been cursing with the hailstorms on Wednesday. Footpaths must have been getting extremely muddy and apparently the moors and low-lying ground was increasingly flooded.

20 February. After the weather it must have been a relief to change the subject. Albert and Jane Champion, a family from Wraxall were celebrating the birth of their daughter Kate their sixth surviving child - the eldest being 15.

4 March. Another birth to celebrate. This time it was a son, Sidney, for James and Jane Hoare an agricultural labourer from Withial. Sidney was their fourth child and who was shown to be shown as 1 month old on the 1881 census forms.

11 March. We think of food scares as being a modern phenomenon but there were at least two during this year, both affecting the poor. In the first there were reports of butter from Ireland being contaminated with poor quality fat that made people ill at the workhouse. The local agent who supplied the contaminated butter was said to be investigating.

The second and larger one was with American bacon and this was sure to have been a topic for discussion by Silas on his round. The local paper in an editorial reports,

'American bacon is an important part of the food of the people of England. We candidly confess that, on account of its cheapness, if not its flavour, we have preferred it in comparison to some home-cured pork. The poor during the last winter could hardly have tasted meat had they not been able to buy this article.'

The problem was that it was contaminated with Trinchinous worms which caused terrible stomach upsets. The worms had been known to survive even half an hour's boiling. It had become a matter of local discussion following the death in

America of a Somerset couple from Burrowbridge who had only emigrated the year before. The French had imposed an import ban but the British Government refused. Isn't it amazing how little things have changed in a century and a quarter? The benefits of locally-produced food still have to be learnt by many!

16 March. The first death of the year would have been discussed with the passing of Rebecca Yeoman aged 84. Given the severity of the weather it is somewhat surprising that there had not been more deaths amongst the elderly. It suggests that neighbours and family did look after them.

25 March. The winter refused to go away. At the weekend it had been beautiful sunshine but on Monday Silas had to suffer snow and rain during his round. There was a sharp frost at night, which must have made conditions slippery under foot, and there were a number of snowstorms following on during the week.

25 March. Silas may have been keen on passing on a story of a gas explosion in the houses at Field View that he would have passed on his way out of Shepton. There was a gas leak that a plumber and boy were trying to locate along the pipe - with a lighted candle! Where were Health and Safety at Work when you needed them? Apparently the boy's face was badly burnt but his sight was not damaged. The plumber only received minor burns.

29 March. The only wedding of the year - but being a farmer's wedding no doubt the festivities were extensive. Annie Cary Gollege (two excellent farming family names from the area) 23 year old daughter of Joseph Gollege of East Pennard, married Charles Biggins 28 son of Joseph Biggins of West Bradley.

1 April. Farmers will have felt considerable relief that markets were able to open again following the foot and mouth restrictions - provided no cattle were bought in from infected areas.

1 April. George Richards of Huxham Farm was announced as the East Pennard Guardian on the Shepton Mallet Union. This was the committee which managed the Workhouse for the Union of Parishes around Shepton Mallet. Each parish had to provide Guardians. Later in the year the Guardians for Stratton on the Fosse at the other end of the Union were prosecuted for not carrying out their role. George Richards was one of the larger farmers of East Pennard and farmers, although not gentry, were quite apparent in responsible roles for the parishes.

4 April. Advertisement. Portman Hotel in the Parish of Pylle close to the Pylle

Railway Station. 'Messrs Moody and Son beg to announce that they will hold their next repository sale at the Portman Hotel on Monday 4 April, for the sale of fat and store cattle, horses, sheep and pigs etc. present entries include 25 rare two and three year old shorthorn heifers the property of Mr J D Allen some with calves at their side, the others nearing calving, a capital Shorthorn Bull of high pedigree, 7 fat heifers, 4 ditto, 3 fresh barreners. The sale of these heifers offers and excellent opportunity to those wishing to fill their dairies with first class animals. They are large of size, good colours and very promising. The greater part are bred by Mr Allen which is a guarantee for breed and quality. Luncheon will be at 12.30 at moderate charge. Sale at 1.30.'

Silas would almost certainly have seen the preparations for the sale as he passed in the morning and no doubt have offered his opinion as to the quantity and quality of cattle to any farmers he saw that morning. Many farmers would have attended the sale - whether they wanted to buy or not. Small sales and markets were very much social occasions where farmers from the area would have met and talked - sales held at public houses with luncheon must have been particularly welcome. That afternoon Silas would have gathered the gossip from the sale on his way back and no doubt it would have provided him with things to talk about for the next few days.

8 April. There may have been a certain amount of speculation over a job advertisement which appeared in the paper. East Compton Farm on the ridge to the north of Pylle was looking for a farm labourer - with a wife to milk preferred. Cottage and good garden found. Liberal wages, apply John J Lewis.

14 April. Although Silas would have been back in Shepton before it started no doubt the next day would have seen comment about the antics of the Shepton Mallet Cycling Club who had an early evening cycle ride to East Pennard, via Wraxall and back via Pilton. Cycling was still a relatively new occupation - presumably it would have been largely the preserve of the 'shopkeeper class'. Not many of the labouring class would have had bicycles at that time. It is also likely that with early cycles and poor road surfaces it would have been very different to the cycling we think of today.

15 April. Withial certainly seems to have been the part of the area for babies. This time it was the turn of labourer James and Elizabeth Parsons for whom Ernest James was their sixth child.

18 April. Easter Monday. The first of the 'cheap excursions' on the railway of the year. This one running to Bath. Though during the year there were many 'specials' to agricultural shows, race meetings or in particular the seaside at

Bournemouth, Weymouth and Seaton. The excursion trains stopped at all the local stations in the morning - including Pylle and returned during the evening. This was a time when the working class were beginning to have an element of disposable income and cheap excursions such as these will have allowed them to visit places their parents would never have dreamt of going. No doubt those who went would have many tales to pass on via the friendly postman the next morning.

21 April. James Dredge, described in the census as a 'farmer and dairyman,' died at the age of 65. This being only a few weeks after the census may explain why at that time his son John Dredge was visiting from London. His daughter Elizabeth was described as a dairywoman.

22 April. It is difficult to know how interested in national news rural people would have been. From the contents of the local paper it is quite possible that they were at least as interested as we are today - possibly more so. There is no doubt however that this week Silas would have found himself discussing the death of Lord Beaconsfield- Disraeli. He had been one of the most noted statesmen of the Victorian age and the papers suggested his death led to a greater national mourning than for anyone since the Prince Consort (Albert, Queen Victoria's husband.)

29 April. The cricket season was getting under way and at this time, like all club sports, cricket was becoming increasingly popular and organized. On his walk up the railway embankment at Townsend in Shepton, Silas will have been watching the erection of a grand new cricket pavilion. Albert Byrt the local stationers and printers were advertising the sale of cricket bats, balls, wickets, leg guards, gauntlets, batting gloves etc etc 'which he can confidently recommend as cheap and durable. Bats from 1s - 30s.' Reports in the paper suggest that most towns (and some villages) now had cricket clubs.

11 May. 'Two performances were given in this town (Shepton) by Ginnett's Circus Touring Company. There was a procession at noon and both at the afternoon and evening performances the large tent was well filled. Many of the country people took advantage of witnessing the feats of equestrianism.' One can imagine that this would have included quite a few who would have walked in from Pylle or East Pennard, perhaps encouraged by Silas's reporting of the circus's arrival.

16 May. There must have been considerable interest in the area as Messrs Moody and Son sold the contents of Cockmill Farm on the western corner of Pylle and northern edge of East Pennard. They were selling the property of Mr E. Dyke who was leaving England - emigration being an option tried by a number of farmers who were frustrated by poor trading conditions in England but who wanted to get on. Many farmers who emigrated discovered that all that glittered was not gold and returned, Dyke is still a very frequently occurring farming name in the area. The sale included all the furniture, from a four poster bed to 2 eight day clocks, a complete set of dairy utensils for cheese and butter making, pigs, horse, harness, casks and much more.

20 May. Both Napiers, father and son, were on the magistrates' bench in Shepton Mallet for a rare local case. Dan Gollege of East Pennard was working on the farm of William Holland in West Bradley and had just sat down for lunch when Mark Green came across the field and attacked him without saying a word. Gollege had not said a word to the defendant and had never had a row with him. Green kept him on the ground kicking him for 25 minutes. It would appear that there had been a previous dispute between Green and Gollege's brother.

Henry Harvey a boy working with Gollege witnessed seeing Green come across the field to Gollege and fall upon him and 'pump it into him.'

'The Chairman said it was a most unprovoked assault for nothing. The defendant had beaten complainant about unmercifully; he would be fined 10s and costs 12s 6d.' The fine represents just over a weeks wages but does seem quite lenient for the severity of the crime.

20 May. 'School Board -The following gentlemen have been re-elected members of the East Pennard School Board. The Rev Adam Goldney, Messrs G B Napier, George Richards and James Dredge. The Board of Guardians will have to elect a new member in the room of Mr Joseph Board who has resigned.'

29 May. There was a baby son - George for single woman Jane Eliza Higgins. It is very difficult to gage how much social stigma would be attached to this. Our popular picture of prim and proper Victorians would imply that the girl would be ruined for life. This doesn't appear to be the case, it was a fairly frequent occurrence which rural families coped with much as they would do today. It is perhaps amoungst the middle classes that the stigma became more significant.

3 June. Although no one in either Pylle or East Pennard was involved there was bound to have been discussion about 10 cases reported before the magistrates this week where parents were fined for their children not attending school. Amongst the reasons given were not being able to afford the fees (only a penny or two a week which could be remitted if they applied to the poor law officers), needing the child to work while father ill, child ill (only accepted with a doctors certificate) or in one case a bad child who refused to go. The magistrates gave a few another chance - where the excuse seemed genuine - but imposed fines of up to 5s in most cases. It should be remembered that it was only 10 years since school attendance had become compulsory and in the main it is obvious that for the vast majority education for their children was something that was appreciated. It is interesting that with the shortcomings of elements of our education system these days, especially in the inner cities, the courts are once again being turned to with the enforcing of the legal obligations on the parents.

8 June. Silas will probably have made a slight diversion to see the events in Parbrook in the south of East Pennard. The foundation stones were laid for the new Wesleyan Chapel which was being erected in the village. An address was given in the afternoon by the Rev James Walter of Yeovil and a public tea was provided at five o'clock 'and of which a good number partook.' A sermon was preached in the evening and collections were made at the end of each service for the building fund.

16 June. The death of a child, although perhaps more frequent in those days, was still always a cause of great sadness and suffering for the parents. Eleven year-old Kate Lye, daughter of George and Jane Lye of Stone at the southern edge of East Pennard passed away. She had three younger sisters Ellen, Mary and Ann.

17 June. Haymaking must work up a good thirst. The local paper saw adverts this week from two breweries.

'Cheap ale for sale, suitable for harvesting. Apply to Sherring & Co Old Brewery Shepton Mallett'

'Old Ale for sale - suitable for farmers use. Anglo Bavarian Brewery Shepton Mallet.'

It may not have been legal to pay wages in beer or cider anymore but its provision at haymaking or Harvest time was still considered essential. Cider would still have been made on many of the farms - but beer would now more normally have been obtained by ordering a barrel from the brewery.

23 June. A cheap railway excursion may well have been enjoyed by a number of local farmers - it went to Salisbury for the Berkshire and Hampshire Agricultural Show.

25 June. Mary Dredge passed away at a very respectable age of 86.

26 June. Frank Lester and his wife Ann who lived in the delightfully named Huckey Mead - the lane beyond Huxham - were celebrating the birth of their fifth child - a daughter Agnes Jane.

1 July. With foot and mouth still rumbling about it was now swine fever which contributed to the perils of farmers and no doubt Silas would have had many conversations on this subject as this week an outbreak was reported at Westcombe only four miles east of Pylle. Three swine had to be slaughtered on the farm of Joseph Taylor and it was thought other animals may have been affected. The premises were declared to be an infected place.

1 July. George Oborne of Pylle appeared on the latest batch of offenders for not ensuring that their children attended school regularly. His wife attended claiming that she had been obliged to keep the girl at home for two weeks as she had a large family including a baby of three months old. The case was dismissed with a caution.

1 July. We get another feel for the weather in an editorial in the paper which was optimistic about the prospects of farming. Apparently there had been rains for the past few weeks and though it may have harmed a bit of clover it had been thought excellent for grass and corn. They now hoped for a few weeks sun to ripen the crops. It was thought that things had begun to look up for farming and pointed out that farmers ought to be supporting the political parties who promised to look after them. One grievance was that diseases that were thought to have been bought in from abroad had hit them hard. A more particular gripe was with the tithes a tax which was thought unfair. In particular it was said to be a landlord tax that should be paid by the landlord and not the farmer. It was another 50 years before this issue was resolved.

6 July. July can be a worrying time for farmers with hay cut when heavy rain may spoil the crop unless it clears up quickly. Their worst fears must have been realized on Tuesday night and Silas must have been quite dubious setting out on Wednesday morning as a tremendous thunderstorm raged. The lightening was described as being exceedingly vivid and one peal of thunder was said to have literally shook the town. Henry Hayward was working trying to thatch a rick of hay at Prestleigh 'when he was struck by lightening and the fluid caused him to spin round several times and then fall heavily from the rick to the ground.' He was conveyed to his home when medical assistance was rendered by Dr B. N. Hyatt of Shepton Mallet. The man lives however in a precarious state."

8 July. Swine fever had spread to Charles Sims at Pilton and William Board at Withial in the parish of East Pennard. Silas may have had to make some arrangements to avoid going on farms with pigs. It was also at Mr Luff's of Rodmoor Farm, Evercreech so appeared to be getting a strong hold in the area.

15 July. The magistrates ordered the shutting of Shepton Mallet market until July 31 following another outbreak of swine fever - this time on the farm of another Mr Luff at Lower Westholme in Pilton. Nine animals were infected and the farm was declared an infected area.

15 July. For Silas it was probably one of the biggest talking issues of the year. A farmer in Shepton Mallet, Mr C Brown, had hired a gang to make hay on the Sabbath. The reaction in the local press was as if Armageddon had occurred. Letters of the strongest language were written and petitions were organized. Apparently huge crowds had gathered to watch the act in disbelief. It was thought that it was typical of the low nature of the inhabitants of Kilver Street that the labourers had come from there.

It was a couple of weeks before Mr Brown was able to put his defence and for the odd more rational voice to point out that there was much work that was done on a Sunday so why was haymaking so villainous? Maybe attitudes were beginning to become more liberal as to what could be done in Sundays but it was obvious that the traditionalists were still very much the dominant force in society.

With all that said, the paper also reports that there had been some excellent hay made.

17 July. Elizabeth Foote of Pylle was buried. She was 82 years old and in the April census had been described as infirm, living with two of her granddaughters.

22 July. July seems to have been one of those months where Silas would have a great deal of news to pass on. The news this week was of an unfortunate drowning in a mill pond in Evercreech of 18 year-old George Hargraves, the son of the schoolmaster. He was swimming with others when he got a cramp. Despite the best efforts of his brother and friends he could not be saved. Controversy, which continued for a number of weeks, concerned the role of the mill keeper who had refused to open the sluices to drain the pond. He argued at the inquest that there had been no point and that he had tried to help. Others hotly denied this.

7 August. Baptism of Arthur, son of George and Annie Oborne. I wonder if this was the belated baptism of the baby which had kept his sister off school?

12 August. The magistrates' court saw the trial of Henry Lister of East Pennard who was charged with shooting a pheasant without a game licence on 27 July. The witness was a 'little boy' William Hatcher of Huckey Mead who had been bird keeping for Mr William Austin Moody. He saw the defendant with a white dog which hunted up the pheasant out of a ditch. The defendant then told the witness to get behind a rick and shot the bird when he was only about 20 yards away. He then threw the pheasant over the hedge to another man who put it into a basket.

John Hatcher, brother to the first witness said he had seen the defendant mowing in a field belonging to Mr Strickland between eight and nine o'clock in the evening. He saw the defendant leave off work and was going home when he took a gun out of the hedge.

The defendant claimed he had never shot a pheasant and that the only bird he shot that day was a wood pigeon.

Captain Ernst (magistrate) said that he had never heard a clearer case in his life and he begged to tell the defendant that for that offence he was liable to be prosecuted by the Inland Revenue Authorities for shooting game without a license and was liable to a fine not exceeding twenty pounds; he was also liable under certain different clauses to be fined for the same offence. He would be fined three pounds plus costs amounting to eleven shillings or in default one month imprisonment with hard labour.

If we compare this to the case of the beating up a farm hand where there was only a 10 shillings fine it does rather make you wonder at the values of the day.

21 August. The shoemaker at Pye Hill, William Pippen, and his wife Elizabeth were celebrating the birth of their fourth child, a daughter, Agnes.

26 August. Due to foot and mouth in adjoining counties the restriction on moving cattle was extended for another month

27 August. Saw the burial of John Close in East Pennard at the age of 81. On the whole they certainly seem to be a long-lived community.

2 September. The never-ending conversation on the state of farming will have taken new twists. After looking so good the harvest had been ruined by rain and even floods through the normally sunny month of August. As this was not a great grain area the local farmers will not have been as badly-affected as in other parts of the country but they will no doubt have had their moan.

2 September. Some good news however. The premises of John Purnell Luff of

Rodmore Farm Evercreech have been declared free from disease following the swine fever outbreak.

7 September. Nearly all the local farmers and many of the farm workers would have gone to the 29th Annual Cattle Show of the Evercreech Farmers Club and Agricultural Association (now the Mid Somerset Show). This was the major local event in the farming year with many farmers showing their cattle or, if not their cattle, then their horses, cheese or butter. This was an era when farmers were keen to show how much they were improving their standards and the show gave them an excellent opportunity - as well as being a huge social event. Cheaper entry was offered after four o'clock and perhaps Silas was amongst the many local people who took advantage of the lower entry rates at the end of the day. I am sure he could have found a friendly farmer of two to stand him a drink.

16 September. The new fashion of the summer had been lawn tennis - which although based upon older games was a new sport. There had been reports earlier in the summer of the first match in Shepton Mallet being played on the cricket field. The neighbouring small village of West Bradley seems to have been the local hub with a club being formed in June with three courts on a field lent by farmer William Pearce. No doubt the antics of the minor gentry and leading farmers caused much comment amongst the population as a whole and the rural postman in particular. The culmination of the season was a grand tournament with prizes for the leading lady and gentleman players. According to the local paper 'A large tent was erected for the occasion and the ground was marked out with numerous flags of red and blue - the club colours- leading to a gay appearance to the scene...... A supply of lemonade and ginger beer was provided in the tent and a substantial tea was tastefully laid out in a large barn...' The Glastonbury town band played for the 200 people attending. The Vicar of Pylle was one of the umpires and, it would seem, the aging Rector of East Pennard was one of the competitors.

23 September. The advertisement for the next repository sale at the Portman Hotel includes notice of the sale of 1 choice bred Guernsey cow and calf. This would still have been quite an oddity in an area where 'cow' was virtually synonymous with 'Shorthorn' The last quarter of the nineteenth century saw considerable advances in the breeding of pedigree cattle - even with the shorthorn. The age of improvement, which had started with the gentry in the late eighteenth century, had filtered down to the 'yeoman' farmer class.

23 September. The birth of a son, Arthur, for local farmers William and Fanny Board.

29 September. East Pennard saw a rather unusual christening that would have done the rounds of gossip. Catherine May Pugh, daughter of Samuel and Elizabeth of Devizes in Wiltshire, was welcomed into the church at the age of 23. Late christenings are relatively unusual but not uncommon. In this case it was made slightly remarkable by the fact that she was a governess. One can imagine that in the rather correct Victorian society discovering that your governess was not christened came as a bit of a shock.

2 October. John Thomas Luke was the rather grand set of names given to the illegitimate son of Elizabeth March a single woman of Pylle.

21 October. Poor old Silas - though at this time he was still in his early 30's - the weather in 1881 seems to have had everything to throw at him in his struggles to deliver the Royal Mail.
'Terrific Gale - What has been described as a fearful hurricane passed over the whole breadth of the British Isles on Friday last doing a tremendous amount of damage both inland and along the coast. In and around Shepton Mallet the severity of the gale was experienced but in a milder degree. The roofs of several houses were dislodged, chimneys were blown down and trees uprooted - but fortunately no accident to any human is reported. A very fine tree at Charlton House succumbed to the terrible force of wind and pedestrianism generally was rendered extremely uncomfortable.'

The beerhouse in Wraxall kept by Mrs Knowle. (postcard H Gifford)

21 October. 'A Sleepy Drunkard.' Richard Humphries, a labourer of Ditcheat was summoned for being drunk and disorderly on the highway at Wraxall. The Ditcheat policeman, PC Billings, followed Humphries into a beerhouse kept by Mrs Knowle where he stood before the fire and started abusing him. The officer told the landlady not to serve him any more beer and she then ordered the defendant to leave. An hour or so later the policeman found Humphries lying on a pile of stones fast asleep. He helped him home. Humphries claimed that although he was not sober he was not drunk and that the policeman hadn't helped him but had pushed him. He was fined 5s

Humphries was obviously a bit of a problem as a few weeks later he was up in court again for abusing his wife.

Mrs Knowle and the beerhouse are also of interest. In the census she appears as Eliza Noyle 67 Innkeeper. However surprisingly it is not the Inn at Stone or the Queens Arms at Wraxall both of which also appear in the census. Adrian Pearse has now identified the beerhouse as the New Inn and provided the photograph. This cottage can still be easily recognized on the road from Wraxall to Ditcheat

28 October. There may have been a certain amount of conversation on Silas's round about a sad affair from a few miles down the Fosse Way at Babcary where 78-year-old Caleb Payne had committed suicide. The old retired butcher had been house bound for some months but left unattended by his daughter for a short time had managed to leave the house and thrown himself down a well where he drowned. The coroner's jury returned a verdict that the deceased had committed suicide whilst in an unsound state of mind.

4 November. It is to be assumed that Col Napier stood down from the magistrate's bench when a case concerning trespass on his land was heard. However it would appear that his son G B Napier was still sitting. William Moody and William Wake were summoned for trespass 'in search of conies' (rabbits). They were seen by PC Hucker, stationed at East Pennard, approaching a rabbit warren. The P C saw them put down two rush baskets in which he discovered three gins (traps) which were later discovered to belong to Col Napier. They were each fined 10s and 7 s costs, "The bench remarking that it was lucky for them they were not charged with theft."

11 November. Advertisement in the paper for a sale of 100 maiden elm and ash timber trees growing on an estate at East Compton. Apply Tennant Walter Haggert to view.

13 November. Silas would have reported on two baptisms at Pylle for children of people who would have been incomers to the parish. Emma Jane was a daughter for groom Charles Griffen and his wife Jane. Francis Kate was a daughter for Thomas Alexander the stationmaster and his wife Jane.

18 November. There must have been considerable merriment in the discussions around the case of Job Robbins who was summoned for not having proper control over a horse and cart. PC Hucker said he was on the main road at East Pennard at around 9.30 in the evening when he saw a wagon loaded with hay drawn by two horses. The wagon was also towing a cart in which appeared to be some sacks. He noticed that there was no one in charge and stopped the horses. Robbins came up a couple of minutes later when it was also discovered that Robbins's father was asleep under the sacks in the cart. Fined 10s as there had been previous convictions.

22 November. Not having been able to identify a cricket club in Pylle or East Pennard the following was a delightful discovery.

'Cricket Dinner' - The annual dinner in connection with the Huxham Green Cricket Club took place at the Queens Arms Inn on Tuesday 22 November where about 30 members and friends sat down to an excellent repast, provided by host masters and upon whom it reflected great credit. Upon the removal of the cloth the usual patriotic toasts were given by the Chairman, and they were enthusiastically drunk by the company. Other toasts of a complimentary character were given and responded to and at intervals during the evening the company were enlivened by the rendering of some capital songs and a most pleasant and enjoyable evening was spent.'

Sounds as if there may have been a few thick heads to greet Silas on the following morning.

5 December. Somerset and Dorset Joint Line Cheap Excursion to Smithfield Cattle Show. Leaving Pylle Monday at 8.20 and returning Wednesday & Thursday. Train excursions to The Royal Smithfield show for farmers and farm workers were a tradition for a long time. Many current farmers can remember going on them. Things come a full circle with the moving of Smithfield to the Bath & West Show Ground for October 2006 - though where the extra curricular entertainment that was a feature of London is going to be provided locally is a question still open!

12 December. Portman Hotel Repository Sale. 'Christmas Beef and Mutton etc. Messrs Moody and Son will give a prize of £2 for the highest price Fat heifer or Cow bona fide sold at the above sale and £1 for the second highest.

16 December. Silas will certainly have been talking to farmers about the good prices for fat stock being reported at the Christmas Markets which might 'encourage farmers to believe that the tide of adversity has begun to ebb.'

16 December. A national story that may have got some local comment this week concerns the sad story of Mr William Powell MP for Malmesbury who was lost in a ballooning accident. The balloon carrying three people from Bath to Bridport tipped up on landing, two were thrown out but the balloon with Mr Powell in it was swept out to sea and not seem again. Mr Powell was a nephew of the cheese factor Mr Cary of the Convent Shepton Mallet and therefore very probably related to the Cary farmers in Pylle.

22 December. Burial in Pylle of Eliza March aged 67. Given the number of the March family in Pylle it is likely that this was well attended by mourners.

23 December. Silas will have been congratulating many farmers on his round who were mentioned as supplying the exceptionally good meat bought by Shepton butchers. They included fat heifers from Mr Norton, Ditcheat Hill, pigs, oxen and a fat calf from Mr Cary at Pennard Hill and heifers grazed by Mr Dredge of Pylle.

30 December. The Shepton Mallet Journal in its round up of Christmas reported. 'The energies of the Postmaster, Mr Coombs, and his assistants were greatly taxed, the receipt of letters through the post being exceedingly heavy. The postman was about four hours late on Christmas morning, but considering the great excess of missives, to the Post Office authorities is due great credit for carrying out so expediently their labourious task.'

One thing is for sure, with the weather, the state of agriculture, births and deaths, and the misdemeanors of the local characters there would have always been plenty for Silas to talk about on his forty years on the round.

Silas - towards retirement

When I carried out my reconstruction of Silas's round I was a bit surprised to arrive in Wraxall at about eleven o'clock. I hadn't started until eight and I anticipated that Silas may well have started earlier than that. Admittedly I had not delivered any letters or covered the diversions that Silas would have. However, it did strike me that he may well have arrived here some time before he was due to go back. I speculated that he must have had an arrangement with one of the local cottagers or the Inn where people could have left letters for him to collect and he could have spent a leisurely couple of hours before it was time to start back.

However Barrie Davis revealed to me that according to family legend as well as being a postman Silas ran another small business as a clock mender. He apparently had a hut in Wraxall which he went to when he arrived there. Further investigation has shown that this appears to have been common practice. George Jasienecki alerted me to a book by Mark Baldwin about Simon Evans. Writing of the interwar period - so perhaps not directly comparable - he says,

"Somewhere near this terminal point the Post Office had provided a rest hut. This was a normal provision for a full-time rural postmen. The hut contained a stove, thus allowing the postman to dry his clothes and rest before walking back to his

Rural postman Charlie Hughes outside the hut in Downhead where he mended shoes
(photo John Reakes)

starting point. While in the hut, the postman could be called upon to fulfil simple Post Office duties, such as selling stamps, and accepting registered letters, licence applications and the like."

Another example much nearer to home then came to light. Charlie Hughes was a rural postman on the Shepton Mallet to Downhead round during the inter war period. Thanks to John Reakes of Doulting we have a wonderful photograph of him standing outside his hut where he mended shoes in the middle part of the day.

Barrie had got firm information on the hut from Cyril England who for many years ran the garage on the cross roads at the bottom of Wraxall Hill. Now sadly semi derelict according to Barry it had been a fine business when Cyril ran it whilst he lived in the large house behind which has recently been improved.

The England family make a number of appearances in this story. The 1901 census shows

East Pennard - Waterfall Cottage (Post Office)

Albert England	27	Sub-postmaster, Groom, Gardener (Domestic)
Cleopatra	29	
Clara	5	
Nelson	2	
Emily	1	
Jane Corp (cousin)	64	

Cyril was another son of Albert. Albert was to fill the role of sub-postmaster for very many years and was succeeded by two daughters (a spinster and a widow) who Barry used to call on for 'the Pearl' in the 1960s. He recalls seeing one of the sisters in hospital after she had been washed away in a flash flood, in July 1968, when the small stream running outside the Post Office rose to unimaginable proportions. The cottage is in a little glen with the stream running beside it. According to the 'Mendip Village Trail of East Pennard' by Penny Stokes, this stream used to have two small waterwheels which were used to pump water to a reservoir for Pennard House a couple of hundred yards away up the hill.

Silas must for the last ten years or so that he was working have seen Albert England virtually every day. He played a part in the celebrations around Silas's retirement. A cutting from the Shepton Mallet Journal 11 October 1908 shows:

'.....the East Pennard sub-postmaster (Mr England) and Mr J Board, one of the principal residents of the village attended to present Mr Davis with a testimonial

Waterfall Cottage 'The Old Post Office' East Pennard
Susie, Jesse and Jennie England pose in front. (postcard Adrian Pearse)

consisting of an illuminated address and a purse of gold from the residents of the district he had so long and faithfully served.'

The family association continued as Albert England and Cyril were amongst the four people from East Pennard listed as mourners at Silas's funeral in 1943.

It was Cyril who pointed out to Barrie where Silas's clock mending was carried out. He pointed it out from his garage in Wraxall as being slightly further down on the same side of the Fosse Way. Near to the single cottage that is still there right beside the narrow part of the road, before the former Police House which is set back on the right.

It is quite possible that Silas just built himself a hut on the wide verge of the ancient Roman road. During the nineteenth century as roads were very gradually improved and surfaced many which had previously sprawled over a wide area were narrowed to a consistent carriageway. It certainly appears that some of the cottages along this stretch of the Fosse, with their long thin gardens running parallel with the road, were built by squatters; the ownership of the grass verges often a very grey area. It is quite possible that Silas may well just have 'borrowed' a bit for his own use.

Barrie found a fascinating story that corroborates this by talking to an elderly client, Mr Birch, who lived in the village of Baltonsborourgh about four miles west of Wraxall. Mr Birch was nearly 100 when he died in the 1990s. Apparently he used to have been a carter come livestock dealer. One day he was passing a farm and the farmer was being 'turned out' and had some of his remaining goods on the roadside. Mr Birch saw a grandfather clock and asked the farmer what he was going to do with it. The farmer said he could have it if he wanted and Mr Birch gave him 12/6d (62p) for it. He put the clock on his wagon and was going towards Ditcheat when he stopped and chatted to an old postman who asked him about the clock and reckoned he had got a good deal. The postman asked him if he wanted it done up and they agreed that he would and see what he could get selling it.

Mr Birch suggests that he hardly gave the clock another thought and forgot about it for eighteen months. One day he when he passing that way again and the old postman came out and called him saying he had something for him - and gave him the twelve pounds he had got for the clock. Mr Birch reckoned that that had been some deal.

The next time Barrie went to visit him he took a photograph of Silas along and Mr Birch immediately identified him as the old postman and clock repairer. The photographer had printed his name on the bottom of the photograph, Frank Higdon of Street. Mr Birch said he thought that he was the photographer who for many years walked around the local countryside taking photos of locals. He also suggested that the photograph may have been taken in Wraxall. It is certainly one that Silas was proud of and a number of copies still exist - I have seen two.

This picture of a dual role of postman and clock repairer helps build our appreciation of the way in rural Victorian England work and lifestyle were sometimes more combined than the sharp distinction we have today. Albert England's census entry showing him as a sub-postmaster, groom and gardener is another example of multiple occupation. Some social historians may suggest that this shows that people had to work their fingers to the bone at every opportunity that came their way to make ends meet but somehow that doesn't feel to have been the case. They may have worked hard but there was an element of independence and self-achievement in what they did. Many other examples of this could be found in the countryside.

The timing of Mr Birch's tale is also not certain. It certainly opens up the possibility that Silas carried on his clock mending hobby/ business in Wraxall after his retirement in 1908. Further evidence of this comes from East Pennard historian Adrian Pearse. I was amazed that when I mentioned Silas Davies he knew that he had the hut on the verge at Wraxall. Adrian had some years ago

A picnic in a field at Huxham to celerbrate the coronation of George V.
Silas is second from the left. (photo Adrian Pearse)

talked history with the late Olive Stone of East Pennard who remembered him. From this source came the delightful photograph of a group in the fields celebrating the coronation of George V in 1911. Olive Stone is one of the two very young girls in the front right. But there sitting second from the left is unmistakably Silas Davis with his Imperial Service Medal on his chest. Although retired and living in Shepton Silas was still undeniably part of the scene in Wraxall and Huxham.

Adrian also pointed out that towards the time Silas retired the motorcar was beginning to make an impact. Wraxall Hill provided particular challenges and organized 'hill trials' were staged up the main road for owners to test the performance of cars. The amazing photograph was first examined in an attempt to find a picture of his hut, we believe it would have been on the verge a little beyond the car parked on the verge on the extreme right of the photo. From the appearance of the cars it is believed that this would have taken place shortly before the Great War.

Silas's wages as a postman rose only very slowly but more rapidly around the turn of the century when real wages and standards of living appear to have been rising across society. At the time of his retirement the post office records give a detailed breakdown of his income. He was then earning 22/- a week or £57/7/8 a year. On top of this he had 6/- a week (£15/13/- a year) for good conduct stripes. An authorized allowance of 21/- a year in aid of boots - presumably an essential allowance if you were walking 17 miles a day! His Post Office uniform was valued at £2/2/6d a year. In addition to this his Sunday Duty pay had averaged £9/11/3d a year for the previous three years and he also received 2/- a week (£5/4/4d a year) for 'Parcel Post Compensation' ' being additional pay for additional work performed.' The parcel post had been introduced in the 1880's and presumably Silas was expected to put the parcels in his sack for delivery along with the letters. For superannuation purposes, Silas's final pay was estimated at £91/4/9d a year.

In early 1908 Silas had a health problem of some sort which led to him being granted early retirement at the age of 59 instead of 60 as was the norm for his role. The Post Office records show his attendance at work over the previous ten years and it appears he may have had some form of recurring problem. He had 16 days illness in 1899, 13 days in 1902, 14 days in 1907 and 67 days in 1908. He actually finished work on the 10th January 1908 but was paid until he retired on 17th March. The records also show that he had 3 days special leave in 1905. He had a medical certificate to confirm he should retire. This would originally have been attached to the records but it is no longer there. As the Post Office granted him a full pension and as Silas received glowing testimonials from them the strong inference would seem to be that the medical cause of his retirement was the result of wear and tear carrying out his work - walking ten times around

The dawn of the age of the motor car. A hill climbing competition at Wraxall
(postcard Adrian Pearse)

GPO

B4793/05

Silas Davis

Rural Postman

Sir

Shepton Mallet

3 April 1905

£70

London

Certified Copy

George Gould

Postmaster

Shepton Mallet

5/4/05

I am desired by the Postmaster General to inform you that the Lords of the Treasury have authorised the payment to the Officer whose name is given above of a Pension of Fifty Seven Pounds Fifteen Shillings & fourpence a year.

The Pension which will be paid by warrant from London takes effect on and from the 11th March 1905

The Treasury award is dated to 31 March 1905

I am Sir

Your Obedient Servant

(signed) By Brookgus Mirahall

for the Secretary

Silas's pension
notification letter

the world must have placed some strain on his body.

In the Post Office records is a copy of a letter from the Treasury Chambers dated 31 March 1908.

'Sir, The Lord Commissioners of his Majesties Treasury have had before them the case of Silas Davis, Rural Postman, Shepton Mallet, which was submitted on the 27th instant; and I am directed by Their Lordships to acquaint you that they have been pleased to award to him a Pension of £57/15/4d. My Lords note that Davis is recommended for the grant of the Imperial Service Medal.'

Barrie Davis has two original handwritten letters, frail and yellowing, which relate to Silas's Pension. One is from the Shepton Mallet Postmaster on 9th April.

"Dear Davis, Your pension has been authorized, the amount is £57/14/4d, to take effect from the 18th March 1908.

I hope you will not be disappointed with the amount & I trust you may be spared to enjoy good health & a well earned rest & continue to draw the pension for the next 30 years.

Yours faithfully George Gould."

Well Silas certainly did continue to draw his pension for the next 34 years! There is also no real question of disappointment as he was awarded a full pension. The amount was slightly higher than his basic wage before retirement and represents 63% of his total last year salary, to put it in modern parlance. There are very few pension schemes which would pay in excess of 60% today. To put it in its context, 1908 was the year that The Liberal Party with their enigmatic Chancellor David Lloyd George in particular were forcing through a radical 'Peoples' budget in Parliament that, amongst other things, paved the way for Old Age Pensions for the first time. These would be for the over 70's only at a level of 5/- a person, but only those who had an income of less than £26 a year would qualify!

Further examination of the Post Office records show that for some reason Silas's case was re-examined the following year and the pension was increased to £59/8/4d.

Silas's retirement received good coverage in the local paper; far more than was usual for the time and I think this shows that Silas was already noted as a considerable local character.

In April 1908 we can read;

"Retirement of the Senior Postman

Mr Silas Davis, one of the best known, and the senior postman in the local service, has just retired at a slightly earlier age than was anticipated, owing to breakdown in health, after a service of close on forty years. His registered mileage for the period of his service goes well into six figures, but the probable actual distance transversed by him on foot on his round exceeds a quarter of a million miles. He joined the postal service under Mr Charles Fudge, who retired long since from that post, and was succeeded by Mr Coombs who was followed by Mr Taylor and Mr Longstaff and now by Mr George Gould. The round served by Mr Davis was that to the extreme southern boundary of the district, at Wraxall and East Pennard, and through flood and tropical heat, snow storm and pelting rain, Mr Davis has been a model of persistent punctuality, and has earned by his cheery courtesy and kindness of disposition, the warmest appreciation from his comrades, and the public whom he served. He will be followed to his retirement by the heartiest good wishes of all who know him that he may long be spared to enjoy the well earned pension which he has been awarded.'

The Shepton Mallet Journal had still not finished with Silas. In June we read the following report:

'Presentation

On Friday evening the postal staff with the postmaster and most of the clerical staff, gathered together in one of the sorting rooms to bid farewell to one of the veterans of the establishment, Mr Silas Davis who has retired after prolonged service on the East Pennard route, and who has been awarded the full pension which it is possible to be earned. Mr George Gould, on behalf of the staff, said that they has asked their old colleague, Silas Davis to be there that night for the purpose of presenting him with an arm chair, subscribed for by his former colleagues in the Post Office, both those of the outdoor and the indoor staff. Mr Davis joined the service in 1869, and when looking through his record that day, it struck him that he, the speaker, was then one year old, and had not been breeched (laughter and applause) when Silas Davis first commenced carrying the mails to East Pennard. He retired from the service in 1908 without having a single black mark, and he went through the whole of that long period of nearly 40 years with an absolutely clean record (applause).

He (Mr Gould) had been through the whole of the district lately to see if there was any means of accelerating the service and in the whole of the district he had

The Imperial Service Medal awarded to Silas in 1908

heard nothing but what was favourable - everybody had a friendly or cheerful word to say on behalf of the postman who had served them so long. He most warmly eulogized the good qualities of their old friend who had served the department with vigilance and fidelity so long, and wished him long life to enjoy his pension. - Mr Shore, one of the postmen, added a few words on behalf of those with whom Mr Davis was immediately connected, and thanked the postmaster for presenting the chair to Mr Davis on their behalf. He thought that it would be more appreciated by the recipient knowing it came from the whole staff (hear, hear), and not from one department only.

Mr Davis, who spoke with considerable feeling, thanked the staff for their great kindness shown to him, and to Mr Gould for his kind words. He should appreciate the present very much. He asked each one of those present to accept from him a copy of his photograph, as a little memento of their service together.

Subsequently Mr Davis was mounted in the chair on the shoulders of four of his comrades, and, the others following in procession, he was chaired to his home where the injunctions of the postmaster, that it was intended that he should put the chair where he could occupy it every day, were renewed. The chair bore the inscription:- Presented to Mr Silas Davis by the postal staff at Shepton Mallet on his retirement from the service, 18th March 1908.'

Even this is not quite the end of the Shepton Mallet Journal's coverage of Silas's retirement. In the 31 July issue we learn that:

'Mr Silas Davis, who recently retired from the Postal Service, has been gazetted to receive the Imperial Service Medal. He lives but a few yards from the only other local holder of the medal, Mr Brownsey.'

King Edward VII had introduced the Imperial Service Medal in 1902 and Silas is believed to be the first Post Office worker in the district to receive it. It was introduced to recognize the clerical and administrative grades of the Civil Service. Civil Servants have always expected to receive their gongs as they still do today. To qualify for an Imperial Service Medal on retirement you had to have given 25 years or more of 'loyal and meritorious service.'

The medal was made of silver and had in the centre the Royal Cypher of Edward VII - this changed with the monarch and from 1920 became an illustration of the head of the monarch as on a coin. Around the centre are the words 'For Faithful Service' in blue enamel and at this time the medal was shaped as a seven-pointed star.

The cutting from the Shepton Mallet Journal of 11 October 1908, which has already been twice mentioned, fills in more details.

"A most interesting gathering took place on Monday evening at the Post Office, when the second Imperial Service Medal which has come to the district, and the first in the Postal Service was presented by the Postmaster, Mr G Gould on behalf of the King, to Mr Silas Davis .... He concluded by reading the following letter which had been forwarded through him to Silas Davies:- "Sir, - I am commanded by the King to transmit to you herewith an Imperial Service medal in recognition of your meritorious service as an officer in the postal service, and I am to request that you that you will acknowledge the receipt of the decoration and will sign the acknowledgement with your Christian name in full - I am yours faithfully R F Raynard" - The reading of the letter was greeted with loud cheers, which were renewed when the Postmaster pinned the handsome medal on Mr Davis's breast."

The same cutting shows something of how he was appreciated by the people on his post round. Mr J Board of East Pennard is reported

"On behalf of 140 subscribers in East Pennard, Pylle, Wraxall and neighbourhood, it was his pleasure to ask Mr Silas Davis to accept the address before them, and also a purse of gold as a slight token of their appreciation of long service faithfully rendered.....

The address was as follows:- This testimonial, together with a purse of money was resented to Mr Silas Davis by the inhabitants of the parishes of East Pennard, Pylle and Wraxall whose names are appended below in recognition of his 38 years' service as postman faithfully and honestly carried out to the entire satisfaction of the Post Office department and the inhabitants of the above named parishes. 137 signatures follow.

Mr Davis, who was very deeply affected, suitably replied, saying his wish was that he could thank every subscriber individually.'

As can be seen from the photograph amazingly the medal has survived and is still a treasured possession of great grandson Barry Davis.

Silas - the last thirty-four years

When Silas retired in 1908 he was still only 58 going on 59. Although ill health had caused his retirement he seems to have made a good enough recovery to lead a long and active retirement - during which it is possible to catch a few sightings of him.

It has already been suggested that there is at least circumstantial evidence that he carried on his clock repairing in Wraxall for some years. Mr Birch's recollections of Silas selling the grandfather clock must have happened to him as a very young man if it was before 1908. Mr Birch's memory of the 'old postman' suggests someone who would have looked a bit more elderly than the photograph we have of a spry and energetic Silas shortly before his retirement. Indeed Cyril England who pointed out to Barrie Davis where Silas's workshop was and his sisters who had memories of him would only have been very young children in 1908 suggesting that they knew him at a later date.

Silas's wife Ann died in 1914 after they had been married for 45 years. The gravestone erected by their children says:

'In loving memory of our dear mother Annie. The beloved wife of Silas Davis who fell asleep in Jesus 16th March 1914 aged 65 years. God's will be done.'

The gravestone is still to be found on the north side of the Shepton Mallet Cemetery. Silas was to be buried alongside her nearly 30 years later.

However, Silas seems to have been one of those people who wasn't without a wife for long. A search of the Shepton Mallet marriage register reveals that on 18 June 1916, 67 year old retired postman Silas Davis married 68 year old widow Mary

Hyatt from Darshill. Mary Hyatt had been born Mary Brimson in 1846 in Cranmore where her father Thomas was an agricultural labourer and can be found on the 1851 census lodging in the house of a widow Elizabeth Cornish and her two sons. Thomas at that time was aged 50, his wife Elizabeth 29, Mary 5 and her sister Martha 2 months. In 1871 the family were living in Shepton Mallet where Thomas was described as a labourer aged 60. Quite why he had aged only 10 years in 20 is unclear. One or other must be wrong. Elizabeth was then 49 and Martha 20 and a younger sister Clara 14. Mary by this time had left home and was working as a servant in Dulcote.

In 1876 Mary Brimson married Isaac J Hyatt in Bristol. Isaac was a boot maker and came from Shepton Mallet where his father, also Isaac, worked in the textile mills, although this Isaac originated in Trowbridge, Wiltshire. By 1891 Isaac and Mary and their four children had returned to Shepton Mallet and were living in Darshill. Isaac was still alive in the 1901 census and working as a self-employed shoemaker.

The marriage of Silas and Mary lasted for nearly 11 years until Mary died aged 80 on 24 February 1927. This time Silas spent even less time letting the grass grow under his feet. There must have been something about marriage that suited him.

On the 11 October 1927 the Shepton Mallet parish register shows 78 year old widower Silas Davis, a retired postman, marrying Mary Ann Shumack a 72 year old spinster.

The history of Mary Anne Shumack can be traced through some of the censuses - although this is no easy task as her name seems to be spelt differently each time; Shumack is definitely not a common local name.

In 1861 we find Mary Anne as the five-year old daughter of James and Eliza Shumack at Charlton to the east of Shepton. James is described as a carter aged 40 who had been born in Martock in the south of the county. His wife Eliza had been born in Shepton Mallet and is described as a 39-year old silk velvet weaver. There are two other children at home Charles seven and Jane five months.

In the 1881 census Mary Anne Shumac is described as a 25-year old 'domestic servant - home from place.' Her father James is a brewer's drayman and as they were in Charlton living next door to Fredrick Berryman of the family who owned and ran the large Charlton Brewery there can be little doubt where James worked. Eliza was still there but the only other person in the household is Kate Shumac a seven-year old grandchild. The parish baptism records show that Kate was Mary Anne's illegitimate daughter, born when she would have been about 18. The census record suggests that Kate lived at home with the grandparents while Mary Ann usually worked away in domestic service. Unusually the baptism record appears to give the father's name as well - a George Oatley who may have been of a family from Wells or Dulcote.

In the 1901 census, Mary 'Shamick' aged 44 is found living as the cook in the Leg Square household of Douglas Mackay a leading Shepton Mallet solicitor. This household comprised of 33-year old Douglas as head, his 67-year old widowed mother and three spinster sisters Emily 38, Mary 36 and Evelyn 34. There was also a visitor, 52 year old Margaret Rawson, and a housemaid, 38 year old Clara. Those of you who may be slightly concerned about poor Douglas living in such a female-dominated household please rest assured. Local historian Len Ware has a photograph of a marquee erected at Bowlish House for the town band to play in at Douglas's wedding a few years later!

Considering their advanced age on marriage Silas and Mary Anne enjoyed an extended time together. Christine Marshman has found a cutting in the Shepton Mallet Journal announcing

'Death. Davis.- On 20 September, 1940 Mary Ann Davis, beloved wife of Silas Davis, aged 85 years.'

It is quite noticeable that Silas's wives always seem to have been 'the ladies at home.' As would seem to have been the accepted norm for those days. Whilst Silas seems to have been a well-known local figure there are no mentions of his wives - even in all the extensive press coverage given to his retirement or his funeral.

A comment in Silas's obituary shows that he had been an active member of the AOF. Nowadays it may not be immediately apparent to all that this refers to the Ancient Order of Foresters. This was one of a number of friendly societies, or benefit clubs that were active in Shepton Mallet in the first half of the twentieth century; others included an Order of Buffalos, an Order of Druids and the Freemasons.

These friendly societies had usually been formed in the 19th century as self-help organizations of the working class. They were largely to provide themselves with sickness and death benefits but some organizations also lent money to members, built halls and encouraged education. Many small towns and villages would have had their own 'club' as locally was seen at Evercreech. However the societies in towns tended to be affiliated to national organizations such as the

Foresters.

From the start they were more likely to represent the craftsmen, shopkeeper and foreman elements of the working class. As is always the case the poorest elements of society are those least able to help themselves. These societies developed quite a social / political aspect with meetings, dinners and other activities. Working class people who made their way onto the town council were very likely to have developed their speaking skills in the friendly societies. Even at the start of WW2 the local paper has reports of their annual meeting held in local public houses where despite food shortages major feasts were provided. Silas would most probably have ensured he made his way to occasions such as these.

It is also possible to catch a glimpse of Silas in a wedding photograph which Christine Marshman had gathered. Christine is descended from Silas by his eldest daughter Emily Jane. We last saw Emily as a ten-year old schoolgirl in the 1881 census but she had left home by the time of that in 1891. In fact she had married in 1890 aged 19, a 23 year old stonecutter named Jonah Axe in Odcombe near Yeovil. As the place of residence for both was given as Odcombe it would be likely that Emily had been in service in one of the big houses or farms in that area although no occupation is shown on the wedding certificate. The latter quarter of the 19th century and the beginning of the twentieth was the high point of domestic servants as the wealth of the population rose. Many girls would have gone into domestic service for a few years before marriage.

Jonah Axe later became a stonecutter at the Doulting quarry - returning the family to the Shepton Mallet area. One of the photographs I have been given shows Silas at the wedding in 1913 of his granddaughter Addie Axe (daughter of Jonah and Emily). Addie married Walter White who came from a well-known local farming family, having a farm at Pylle from which he sold milk on the streets of Shepton Mallet. From Pylle they moved to Glenfield, at Haselbury Plucknett, his son Ken then continued running the farm to be joined in turn by his son Roger who after 35 years of farming accepted the role of running the Farmers Markets at Wells, Glastonbury, Wincanton, Yeovil and Crewkerne.

From the same line there is another surviving great granddaughter of Silas, Christine's cousin Mildred Wickham who lives in the same road in Shepton as Barrie Davis. Mildred can remember Silas well from her childhood in the 1930's. They lived in Commercial Road and her father got on well with his grandfather Silas so they frequently walked down Zion Hill to visit him. As you walked down Zion Hill the doorways of the three Crown Cottages were often open and frequently Silas would be waiting in the doorway to catch someone to talk to. She remembers him as a very friendly old man, always chatting. The last time she can remember seeing Silas was soon after the start of the war when her father (Percy

Wedding of Silas's grand-daughter Adelaide Axe to Walter White 1923.
Silas is second from the right. (photo Christine Marshman)

Axe) had been very badly injured in a hit and run accident. Silas made the walk up the hill to visit and she can remember him sitting down and stretching out his legs groaning that the walk had made them ache. In her living room a colourful cup and saucer with a Chinese illustration are displayed. This is the cup that Silas used to drink from which he gave to her father and he in turn passed it on to her - an amazing link to the past.

The 1901 census shows Silas and Ann living already living in Crown Cottages. At home at that time were his youngest son Ernest who was still only 16 and second daughter Annie who was then 27 and a shop assistant (china and glass). Annie was to make an interesting marriage and became quite a significant figure in her own right in the Shepton Mallet community.

John Byrt Godfrey came from a farming family at Lyng on the Somerset Levels. In the early years of the 20th century he took on the tenancy of one of the Duchy of Cornwall farms in Shepton Mallet at Lower Downside. He was related by his first marriage to other local farming families like the Haggetts and Orams. After his first wife died family ledgend has it that John Godfrey was in the High Street of Shepton Mallet when he saw Annie decorating a window in Bowden's shop. He went straight into the shop and asked her to marry him!

A significant local farmer, John Godfrey was throughout the interwar years an energetic chairman for the Mid Somerset Agricultural Society which organized

John and Nancy (Anne) Godfrey pictured with the Prince of Wales in 1935
(photo Christine Marshman)

Silas (extreme right) medal on chest at the Garden Party at Downside following the Prince of Wales's visit in 1935 (photo Christine Marshman)

the annual 'Shepton Show'. By the early 1930s the Shepton Mallet Journal was crediting him with being the person who kept the society running through the 1920s when it would otherwise have folded. Annie and her two step daughters Lucy and Florrie Godfrey are remembered as being extremely active in their work at the show. It was they who produced huge floral arches over Cannard's Grave Road at Field that spanned the entrance to the show.

One of the features of Duchy of Cornwall farms is the interest in which the Prince of Wales of the times shows in them. Our current Prince of Wales is certainly no exception to this, nor was his great uncle who was later to abdicate as Edward the VIII over his marriage to Mrs Simpson. A number of photographs survive of visits he made as Prince of Wales to John Godfrey's farm at Downside. It is at one of these that we can be confident that Silas had at least a fleeting contact with royalty. After the Prince's visit in 1934 there is a photograph taken at a garden party at Yew Tree Farm, Downside, showing the Godfrey family and officials of the Mid Somerset Show. On the right of the photo a very cheerful Annie Godfrey can be seen sitting in a cane chair. Behind her to the right is Silas looking very fit and spry for someone who at that time was about 85. Close examination of the photograph shows that on his lapel he is proudly wearing the Imperial Service Medal he was awarded 26 years before. Mildred Wickham can remember that her mother went to serve the tea and sandwiches at Downside for this garden party.

Gorman, Graham and Barrie are grandsons of Silas's youngest son Ernest who the 1901 census shows as a 16-year old carpenter and joiner. In one of those amazing historical co-incidences Gorman was having some work done on his house in Whitstone Road, Shepton Mallet. When some of the floor boards where lifted to get at some pipes a piece of wood was found and on the back was penciled EH Davis. His grandfather had been a carpenter on the house when it had been built.

Ernest had also worked for the Post Office for a spell in his younger days. There is a fantastic photograph of him riding a bicycle in period postman's uniform. Apparently all of this line of the family have worked either for the Post Office or the telephones, one and the same until the 1970s, however in each case it was for a relatively short time and none of the others made it their career. Gorman had started as a telegram boy, but after the war he found out that he could earn more in the new Clarks shoe factory and made the switch - nearly 60 years later he is still not 100% sure whether this was the right move.

Ernest's wife kept a shop at Victoria Grove in Shepton Mallet, then the family moved to Bristol where they kept another shop. This was where his son Bernard was bought up. This was a family where there was great sadness as Bernard and his two sisters all had tuberculosis. Only Bernard survived. He was an electrician who worked on telephone exchanges. His family with his three young sons Gorman, Graham and Barrie were caught in the German bombing blitz on Bristol early in World War Two. Gorman in particular has horrific memories of the blitz when he says he was so frightened that he lost all control of his bodily functions. Bernard brought his family back to Shepton Mallet where they struggled to find accommodation because of the wartime shortage in the town. However they eventually established themselves and have, by and large, been here ever since.

Although he had been to Shepton before it is from this time that Gorman has the clearest memories of his great-grandfather. He has the idea that Silas was a bit of a rascal - who like all men who live until their nineties only did so on a diet of drinking and smoking. Silas is reputed to have hardly ever missed a session in the Crown Inn next door to him; though this was a very smart and respectable pub in those days. Silas's obituary recalls how he used to walk up town to the Constitutional Club and tell the stories of his time on the post round; it was 'a rare treat to catch him in reminiscent mood.'

Gorman can remember sitting in Crown Cottage with Silas. It was quite magical watching Gorman who is nearly 80 impersonating Silas as an old man of over 90. Getting a short clay pipe from his rack on the mantelpiece where he had one for every day of the week. Hunching himself into the corner of his chair - was this the chair he was presented with on his retirement? - Cutting off a length of his shag tobacco and rolling it in his hands as he looked at Gorman from behind his bushy grey beard. Pushing the tobacco into the bowl of his pipe before lighting it and the wreaths of smoke making their way around the small living room where Silas was surrounded by clocks.

There was no long decline for Silas who, I was told, had not suffered a days illness until one day he was out for a walk and he slipped on some cobbles not far from his cottage. He was taken home but had caught a chill and pneumonia set in. As for so many old people even today the onset of pneumonia is the end and so it proved to be for Silas. He was taken to Rowden House, the hospital and former workhouse in Wells where he died. His long and remarkable innings coming at last to the inevitable conclusion.

Bibliography

Having read numerous books over many years it is difficult to be sure where various snippets of information have come from. However below are the sources I am conscious of referring to for this history.

Shepton Mallet. A Historical and Postal Survey. Eric H Ford. Privately published 1958

A Shepton Mallet Camera. Fred Davis. Shepton Mallet Amenity Trust 1984

East Pennard Village Trail. Penny Stokes, Mendip District Council.

Rural Life in Victorian England. G E Mingay. Lund Humphries 1976

Old Mendip. Robin Atthill. David and Charles 1964

Labouring life in the Victorian Countryside. Pamela Horn. Gill and Macmillan 1976

The Myth of the Great Depression 1873 - 1896. S B Saul. Macmillan and Co 1969

The Victorian Farmer. David J Eveleigh. Shire 1991

Somerset Farming, 100 years of Change. David Walker, Somerset Books 2001

A Town Alive. Alan Stone. Shepton Mallet Local History Group 2004

Shepton Show. Alan Stone. Mid Somerset Agricultural Association 2002

Seasons of Change. Sadie Ward. George Allen and Unwin 1982

Simon Evans his life and later work. Mark Baldwin. M & M Baldwin 1992

In addition much reference has been made to

The Shepton Mallet Journal

National Census' 1841, '51, '61, '71, '81, '91, 1901

The Various Trade Directories for Shepton Mallet published during the nineteenth century.

Acknowledgements

Many people help with a project of this nature. I hope I remember most but apologies to those I forget.

First thanks must go to Silas's great grandchildren, Barrie and Gorman Davis for their memories and in particular Christine Marshman who has been so active in chasing down the certificates relating to family history. Also to Mildred Wickham and step-grandson John Godfrey.

Help has been most generously given by fellow local historians. Adrian Pearse in particular and also Fred Davis, Allen Cotton and Richard Raynsford.

Christine King in Shepton Mallet Library and the staff in Wells Library, the Local Studies Library in Taunton and the County Record Office are always helpful.

The staff at the Post Office archive in London who fortunately managed to work out their own indexing system when I failed.

For proof reading and suggestions I owe a huge debt to Adrian Pearse, George Jasienecki and Brian and Pam Neil. As I tend towards the dyslexic they have their work cut out.

For photographs to Adrian Pearse, Barry Davis, Christine Marshman, John Reakes, Janet Moore and Fred Davis I owe a huge debt of gratitude.

Last but by no means least my family. Sons, history students Richard and James, who are always willing to be critical of the efforts of their father, and my wife Christine who does so much of the investigation into census and parish records for me as well as dropping everything to give a first read through to every chapter as I produce it.

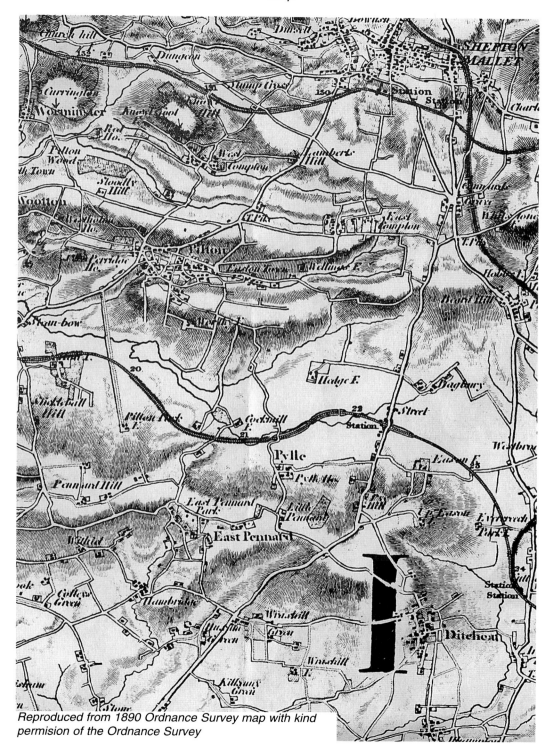

*Reproduced from 1890 Ordnance Survey map with kind
permision of the Ordnance Survey*

Silas in retirement

Index